Thackeray's Novels

A Fiction that Is True

JACK P. RAWLINS

Thackeray's Novels

A Fiction that Is True

University of California Press

Berkeley • Los Angeles • London

University of California Press
Berkeley and Los Angeles, California

University of California Press, Ltd.
London, England

ISBN: 0-520-02562-8
Library of Congress Catalog Card Number: 73-84393
Printed in the United States of America

To
RALPH WILSON RADER,
who taught me books, and
C. BENSEL RAWLINS,
who taught me everything else

Contents

Preface

Frequently an author at the beginning of his career uses parody to define his distance from his predecessors. Thus Jane Austen writes *Northanger Abbey* and Fielding writes *Shamela* and the opening passages of *Joseph Andrews,* purifying the reader of erroneous reading habits and clearing a way for an alternative aesthetic; parody implies an alternative of greater value to the object parodied. In this view, Thackeray is a parodist whose alternative aesthetic is never made clear. His career begins in parody and ends in parody; his statement is always made in terms of the narrator's dissent from an exaggeratedly conventional plot structure within the novel, but he never frees his meaning from a dependence on that artificial structure. Each novel is in large part a restatement of a basic aesthetic dissatisfaction, a turning away from the stuff of the novel itself, but Thackeray remains in search of something of surer value toward which to turn. The aim of this study is twofold: to determine the basis for Thackeray's rejection of contemporary fiction, in order to understand his inability to dispense with the framework of convention and to realize the implicit alternative; and to analyze the narrative methods by which Thackeray's dissatisfaction with his own plot's aesthetic is presented. Chapter 1 examines *Vanity Fair* in order to clarify the difficulties of Thackeray's fiction; chapter 2 seeks explanations aesthetic and philosophical for the state of the novel's text, using Thackeray's critical essays and early fictional experiments as primary sources; chapters 3 and 4 examine the narrative techniques of the later novels (*The Newcomes* primarily); and chapter 5 searches within the last novels (*The Virginians* and *Philip*) for the elements of an aesthetic secure from parody.

Henry James tells us that "as the picture is reality, so the novel is history. That is the only general description ... that we may give of the novel." To "admit that the events he narrates have not really happened" is for the novelist the "betrayal of a sacred office."[1] Throughout our discussion we will find the center of Thackeray's dissatisfaction with the novel as he finds it to be exactly this assertion of James'; for if either the novel is history or it is nothing, an honest rationalist must observe that it is not history, but rather fiction, and, while it may yet be more than nothing, its value is certainly in some doubt. James, in Thackeray's view, locates fiction's value in a lie — the lie that it is true. Thackeray's career is a

[1] "The Art of Fiction," in *The Future of the Novel*, ed. Leon Edel (New York: Vintage, 1956).

search for a fiction that retains its validity when that lie is revealed.

The edition of Thackeray's works used is the Kensington Edition, Charles Scribner's Sons, New York, 1903; but, since there are countless editions of Thackeray and none is regarded as definitive, references to Thackeray's works will give both chapter and page in the Kensington Edition, thus: [*VF* 12; 1:160], meaning, *Vanity Fair*, chapter 12; volume 1, p. 160 of the Kensington Edition.

1: *Vanity Fair:*
The Structure
of Self-Refutation

Vanity Fair is a work of disturbing complexity of structure and style. We are going to try to come to an understanding of that complexity by attempting to fit the book into some established generic forms of narrative fiction, to observe how it refuses to fit, and ultimately to account for the reasons for that refusal. Our question is: How fully can *Vanity Fair* be described as a dramatic action, an apologue, or a satire?[1]

Vanity Fair as Dramatic Action

Vanity Fair certainly wears the face of a dramatic action. It contains the materials of dramatic interest common to novels of Thackeray's period: love unprofessed, poverty unrelieved, and so forth. The elements of the plot are so completely familiar to us as the elements of sentimental romance that we assume that they are being used in the way

[1] These categories are defined by Sheldon Sacks in *Fiction and the Shape of Belief* (Berkeley and Los Angeles: Univ. of California Press, 1964).

of that conventional art form, which is the way
of dramatic action. But things are not so simple.
A dramatic action, as distinguished from a satire
or apologue, seeks to heighten our sympathetic
involvement with a set of characters and a situation
and win from us the strongest possible commitment
to a particular dramatic outcome. There are several
ways in which Thackeray does the opposite of this.
For instance, though readers have testified to the
unique realness of his characters,[2] the compelling
immediacy of their presentation, the narrator tells
us frequently that they are not real, that they are
puppets, and that this is all a kind of light entertainment. If the dramatic experience is premised
upon a willing suspension of disbelief, then Thackeray's methods are designed to reawaken that disbelief, or at least to make us conscious of the wilful
act and examine the criteria by which it is wilfully
done. The effect of the puppet metaphor in this
context is that, if we take the narrator at his word,
the work must be an apologue, where, as in a fable,
the characters are vehicles for truths more important than themselves. But Thackeray's characters
refuse to accept such second-class citizenship. The
significant fact about the puppet metaphor is, after
all, that it is constantly belied by the puppets'
vitality. The drama compels us to a concern for
them which the narrator assures us is foolish and
based on the misconception that they are real. The
metaphor is powerful because it is not how we
perceive the characters naturally. Here, then, is an

[2] Cf. chap. 3 for a complete discussion.

example of a fact to which we shall be constantly returning in this chapter in larger terms: that the force of Thackeray's narrative and his narrator's perception of it are harshly at odds, in that the narrative is trying to achieve fulfillment as compelling drama, and the narrator denies it that satisfaction, by a number of techniques that we will now examine.

But first a cautionary note should be sounded. We are going to talk about the contradictory forces of sentimental drama and an artistic self-consciousness that largely destroys the illusions on which dramatic involvement is based, and this raises a problem. Thackeray writes with a hypothetical reader very much in mind: one of that reader's characteristics is an intense desire for a strong dramatic experience — Victorian novel-readers are historically famous for reading in hopes of a good cry. Only with such a desire will one feel the full effect of Thackeray's refusal to grant it to us. The conclusion of *Vanity Fair* is meant to gall and frustrate. Those who feel that ending to be otherwise must try to reconstruct Thackeray's reader — the reader who reads to weep, the reader who could read Bulwer's ending to *Great Expectations* with no sense of inconsistency. Only then will we realize that the marriage of Dobbin and Amelia remains a consummation devoutly to be wished long after Thackeray has logically demonstrated the unfeasibility of it.

In a dramatic action, the author must clarify our commitment to certain possibilities of action and against others, so that he may control our

dramatic involvement and give us a coherent experience. Does Thackeray seek such a unified effect? Let us follow the progress of the rhetoric
through a representative passage — Dobbin's battle
with Cuff, the school champion [*VF* 5].

Cuff is presented as the representative of all the
social forces that bring Dobbin undeserved con-
tempt and misery. Dobbin is found reading the
Arabian Nights, that traditional sign of unworldly
idealism and the powers of fancy. The world intrudes: "Dobbin looked up. The Fairy Peribanon
had fled into the inmost cavern with Prince Ahmed:
... and there was everyday life before honest William: and a big boy beating a little one without
cause" [p. 62]. Cuff's victim is the very boy who
brought Dobbin shame by revealing his father's low
occupation. The stage is set for an unambiguous
confrontation between ideal virtue and worldly
wickedness; Dobbin will be likened in the next lines
to David against Goliath. Dobbin performs, but the
narrator's speculations about his motives are not
comforting to our dramatic alliances:

> I can't say what his motive was. Torture in
> a public school is as much licensed as the knout
> in Russia. It would be ungentlemanlike (in a
> manner) to resist it. Perhaps Dobbin's foolish
> soul revolted against that exercise of tyranny:
> or perhaps he had a hankering feeling of re-
> venge in his mind, and longed to measure
> himself against that splendid bully and tyrant,
> who had all the glory ... in the place. Whatev-
> er may have been his incentive, however, up
> he sprang..., [p. 62]

Even though we may feel ourselves able to thread our way through the irony and arrive at a probable judgment being hit at here, the act of struggling, the need to pause, and the possibility of ignoble motives are all damaging to the making of a clear and strong dramatic commitment. Dobbin has done the right thing, but the narrator has asked too penetrating a question. The conventional character of the situation, and the conventional rhetoric in which Thackeray narrates it (Arabian Nights, David and Goliath, and so on) encourage a view of the event as a moral dichotomy — David vs. Goliath, Arabian Nights idealism vs. a cruel reality, awkward virtue vs. superb arrogance; the interruption by the speculative narrator destroys the simple purity of the categories — there is some Cuff in Dobbin, for instance. Rhetoric (and here conventionality of plot action must be included in that term) has lied, by encouraging us in a too easy moral response that the objective critical spirit of the narrator easily exposes.[3] This pattern describes every part of Dobbin's experience. Consider the familiar shape of the complete action: Dobbin

[3] It is interesting to note that Thackeray's interruption is, in terms of dramatic characterization, basically misleading. There is, after all, no Cuff in Dobbin. Dobbin can be foolish, but never cruel or vengeful. Since the interruption is not helpful in understanding Dobbin, and is in fact misleading, we cannot explain the interruption in terms of dramatic necessity. That is, Thackeray is not interrupting to correct our dramatic involvement, but simply to disrupt it, without factual cause, and as a matter of policy — pure dramatic situations must be disrupted, just as smooth water cries out for a stone to be thrown in it. Our "too-easy moral response" is in this case accurate, and it is the "exposure" of that view which proves ultimately false. The interruption is false for Dobbin, but true for mankind, and it is this sort of narrative structure, in which the particular dramatic present has only secondary validity, that we are attempting to characterize.

fights in defense of one who has wronged him,
against physical odds and in the face of prejudice.
He wins, winning respect and popularity in the
process. Cuff acknowledges his crime and accepts
the blame for the fight ("It's my fault, sir. . . . I
was bullying a little boy; and he served me right").
Cuff becomes Dobbin's tutor. Dobbin becomes the
best friend of the youth he defended, who helps
Dobbin's father prosper by bringing him socially
respectable patronage. Dobbin gains self-confi-
dence, academic success, and his father's respect.
His father's economic success leads to his becoming
an alderman, and Dobbin's career as a gentleman
is assured. Only by recognizing the complete conventionality of the plot can we appreciate the effect
of the narrator's cynical re-interpretation of it. He
tells us, for instance, that Dobbin's popularity is
for the wrong reasons; he is cheered not because
he is right, but because he wins, and the cheers
smack of hypocrisy — "Now all the boys set up
a shout for Figs as would have made you think
he had been their darling champion through the
whole battle." Cuff's self-abasement proves a cunning bit of politics, winning him back all his lost
status. George Osborne's letter to home shows that
he has failed to catch the moral of the experience;
in fact, Dobbin's damsel in distress turns out to
be a whore, who loves and seeks the ravishment,
for George would always rather be abused by
wealth and blood than befriended by common
virtue.

But Thackeray sees deeper than this, for Dobbin
himself fails to comprehend the moral nature of

his experience. Cuff tutors Dobbin, but the narrator emphasizes not Cuff's condescension but Dobbin's astonishment at it. He feels himself unworthy of such companionship, which makes us distrust the morality in whose defense he fought. Dobbin's father rewards him as much for his associates as for his character, and he pays him in public and in cash, the coin of the realm we thought Dobbin was opposing. Dobbin's self-enslavement to George, the representative of the worst elements of the system he began by battling so heroically, completes his capitulation.

This is something other than a dramatic outcome against our wishes; this is rather a reinterpretation of a dramatically perfect pattern, to the destruction of all clear dramatic commitments. Since what we called Virtue has enrolled in the service of what we called Worldliness, we are left with nothing that we may surely hope for. But the perfection of the conventional plot structure — familiar to all readers of Victorian young men's literature, a genre now known only by its best, Hughes' Tom Brown books — is what we are likely to overlook. Amelia's history as a whole is the exercising of a cynical insight upon a conventional romance. The bare plot summary shows no signs of a revolutionary aesthetic: Downright, honest D meets A and loves her at first sight. But A loves D's best friend G. Her family is ruined, and the match is broken off by G's worldly father. G defies his father, insists on honoring his love for A, and is banished from the family. D, sacrificing his own love, arranges a marriage between G and A. The young husband is heroically

killed in the defense of England's liberty. She vows
eternal loyalty to his memory. D is stationed in
India. A suffers from poverty, unbeknownst to D.
But the cruel father-in-law is reconciled at the sight
of his grandson, so like his dead son, and promises
to provide for him in a gentlemanly manner. D
learns of her poverty, rescues her, wins her love
through years of devoted service, and they are wed.
Surely, few of us read works of such unflinching
ordinariness.

Amelia's plot is as conventional in its parts as
in its whole. Let us take the time to document one
example of the conventions in which Thackeray
openly works. When Dobbin first sees Amelia, he
is love-struck in the manner of a Victorian convention [*VF* 5; 1:70-71].

> He had arrived with a knock so very timid and
> quiet, that it was inaudible to the ladies up
> stairs: otherwise, you may be sure Miss Amelia
> would never have been so bold as to come
> singing into the room. As it was, the sweet fresh
> voice went right into the Captain's heart, and
> nestled there.

The bird imagery ties this to the convention by
which love or sex erupts at any instant of unguard-
ed proximity to nature. In Victorian novels, people
only go outside for proper or improper sexual purposes. Some examples will suggest the universality
of this belief: In *Coningsby*, Coningsby loves Edith,
but lacks an opportunity to declare himself until
they are caught in a rainstorm and take refuge in
a fishing cottage. Two paragraphs of nature de-

scription — such as, "a soft breeze came dancing
up the stream," — and it fairly bursts out of him —

> "Edith!" he said in a tone of tremulous passion,
> "Let me call you Edith! Yes," he continued,
> gently taking her hand, "let me call you my
> Edith! I love you!"
>
> She did not withdraw her hand. [Bk. 7,
> chapt. 5]

Once outside the bounds of civilized society, there
is no hesitating. In *A Blot in the 'Scutcheon*,
Browning uses the convention to explain the paradox that two perfectly innocent and sexless young
people have fallen. Mertoun illicitly loves Mildred,
and the following is all the explanation we ever
get of how they fell:

> *Tresham*: Have you seen Lacy Mildred, by the
> way?
> *Mertoun*: I ... I ... our two demesnes, re-
> member, touch;
> I have been used to wander carelessly
> After my stricken game: the heron roused
> Deep in my woods, has trailed its broken wing
> Through thicks and glades a mile in yours, —
> or else
> Some eyass ill-reclaimed has taken flight
> And lured me after her from tree to tree,
> I marked not whither. I have come upon
> The lady's wondrous beauty unaware.
> And — and then ... I have seen her.
> [*Act 1: 2; 155-164*]

The source of the convention in the Actaeon myth

is explicit here. For a final example, in *Tom Brown at Oxford*, Tom discovers his love through a moment's contemplation on the Hawk's Lynch, a promontory (chap. 32), his friend Hardy declares his love there (47), and Tom's love is first reciprocated in a nature outing which Hughes introduces wittily with, "Has any person, of any nation or language found out and given to the world any occupation, work, diversion, or pursuit, more subtly dangerous to the susceptible youth of both sexes than that of nutting in pairs?" (34). Hughes is joking at the convention he is about to use, joking at the fact that every reader knows why he is sending his young people out nutting.

Dobbin's fall for Amelia, then, is offered to us in terms so familiar that we cannot question it, except through hindsight later. Thackeray then forces us to question it with a basic technique of the parodist — he takes the convention literally, and finds it literally foolish. He sensibly suggests that he who falls in love at first sight falls in love with superficialities. The observation questions not only the grounds for Dobbin's love, but the grounds for our easy countenance of it. But the power of that turn on the convention depends on our accepting it initially as rhetorically persuasive. We must realize that there is an entire conventional romance within this book — we must come to understand how an intelligent reader could say of reading *Vanity Fair*, "I rejoice to read again a good old-fashioned love story"[4] — so that we may recog-

---

[4] Thackeray's *Letters*, 2:313.

nize the means by which Thackeray makes it into something else.

If we return to the Dobbin-Cuff fight, we may note another way in which the narrator's methods seem hostile to the ends of drama. Again, Dobbin has been roused from dreams and is confronted by injustice. The reader who takes a strong stand with Dobbin and against Cuff finds this done to him:

> ... there was everyday life before honest William; and a big boy beating a little one without cause. . . .
>
> "Take that, you little devil!" cried Mr. Cuff, and down came the wicket . . . on the child's hand. — Don't be horrified, ladies, every boy at a public school has done it. Your children will do so and be done by, in all probability. Down came the wicket again; and Dobbin started up. [*VF* 5; 1:62]

Thackeray invites the reader to make moral alliances, and then shows him how he has condemned himself. Such an interruption upsets our dramatic involvement in two ways: first, by picturing us wielding the wicket, and suggesting that the victims and the bullies are the same people at different ages, it confuses our moral stand considerably; but of equal interest, by generalizing the action to all boys in all schools at all times, it weakens our interest in drama's primary end — the illusion of intense and particular reality. The issue is, which is first in importance, Cuff and George, or the condition of the English public schools; this is the difference between a dramatic and an apologic

orientation. The plight of Pamela, to take a clear
example, does not need, nor would it profit by, any
attempt to validate her experience by reference to
its representativeness. Though Richardson suggests that it is "about" Virtue Rewarded, we are
not misled; it is fundamentally "about" Pamela
and Mr. B, who testify to their own existence and
significance by themselves, as unique creatures.
Thackeray's interruption corrects our inclination
to read the scene this way and directs us toward
an apologic orientation.[5]

Vanity Fair as apologue

An apologue, according to Sacks, is "a work
organized as a fictional example of the truth of
a formulable statement or a series of such statements" [p. 26]. We can immediately see that *Vanity
Fair* advertises itself as an apologue. Here, as in
all his works, Thackeray habitually refers to his
art as fable, or sermon, often with a blunt statement that our response to the text should be to
take the moral. Here the moral is repeated often

[5] Sacks brings light here. He discusses the ways Dr. Johnson mini-
mizes our involvement in *Rasselas'* episode of the stoic and his
daughter's death; he speaks of Imlac's generalization to Rasselas about
such men — "Be not too hasty . . . to trust, to admire, the teachers
of morality: they discourse like angels, but they live like men": "What
is most important about Imlac's prediction at this moment is its
generality. . . . Since the genuineness of the wise man's grief is conveyed
by careful contrast to the spuriousness of his moral dicta, it is absolutely necessary that we regard meretricious pretensions as typical of
"teachers of morality," since for purposes of the apologue the pretensions of a single moralist are irrelevant. Imlac's brief rejoinder at once
reinforces our propensity to find in the episode only its thematic
contribution . . . and prevents us from interpreting the seer's
spuriousness as idiosyncratic" (p. 58).

— *Vanitas vanitatum*, all is vanity — and the novel apparently ends when it is felt that the truth of this has been fully demonstrated. Thackeray in his letters describes his purpose as the description of the moral state of a society, not the telling of a story; he says, "What I want is to make a set of people living without God in the world. . . ." [*Letters* 2:309] And Thackeray throughout his career describes the relationship between reader and text that he seeks by the phrase *de te fabula*, meaning that the reader is the subject of the tale. Our attention is thus ultimately directed, not toward Cuff and Dobbin, not toward the universal fact of such things happening, but toward the fact that we have done it. That the novel appears to be about fictional characters in action proves to be an illusion; the novel begins to look like a grand rhetorical machine to bring the reader unawares face to face with himself. In this perspective the Cuff-Dobbin fight seems a trap laid to encourage us to make pure moral judgments which turn out to condemn us, and to leave us to resolve the conflict. This is a joke fundamental to Thackeray's method, and it, like much of his humor, is based on the difference between the way we read and the way we live. We read romantic novels with an easy moral absolutism and live according to a more pragmatic creed. By casting us as the characters of his novel, Thackeray asks us to account for the discrepancy.

But the machinery of apologue that *Vanity Fair* sports is not conclusive evidence that an apologic intention is controlling the structure of the novel.

As Sacks observes, the error to demand or assume
an apologic orientation is historically a common
one in talking about the novel, especially so for
Thackeray's generation; from the time of Defoe if
not earlier, the novelist has found it convenient
to "mistake" his creation for an apologue, as the
best defense against moralist critics who demand
of it some demonstrable moral "use." The claim
to a moral purpose, and the pose as preacher or
parabolist, are necessary features of the Victorian
novelist's public image.[6] And since one of Thackeray's main interests is the proper function of the
novelist, and since he likes to joke that his art is
alternatively more serious and less serious than the
archetypal "novel," his claims to an apologic power
cannot be valued highly without corroboration in
the experience of the novel itself. But *de te fabula*
is more than machinery; it describes the only way
in which a large part of *Vanity Fair* can be read.

Thackeray's new orientation shows clearly in his
death scenes, because here we expect the dramatist
to seek the most intense concentration on the
dramatic here and now. The almost indelicate
submersion of self in the texture of the death scene,
which we expect from Victorian novelists, is described by Fitzjames Stephen with characteristic
lack of restraint: Dickens "touches, tastes, smells
and handles it [death], as if it were some savory
dainty which could not be too fully appreciated."[7]
Though we would want to quarrel with some of

[6] Cf. Richard Stang, *Theory of the Novel in England, 1850-1870* (New
York: Columbia Univ. Press, 1959), p. 68.
[7] Stang, p. 62.

the implications of this, it accurately reflects the
reader's sense of an intense involvement with the
physical situation. Thackeray attends to different
aspects of the experience — with the death of Mr.
Sedley, for instance [*VF* 61; 3:229ff.].

> There came a day when the round of decorous
> pleasures and solemn gaieties in which Mr. Jos
> Sedley's family indulged, was interrupted by
> an event which happens in most houses. As
> you ascend the staircase of your house . . , you
> may have remarked a little arch in the wall
> right before you, which at once gives light to
> the stair which leads from the second story
> to the third . . . and serves for another purpose
> of utility, of which the undertaker's men can
> give you a notion. They rest the coffins upon
> that arch. . . .
>
> That second-floor arch in a London house
> . . . what a memento of Life, Death, and Vanity
> it is . . . if you choose to consider it, and sit
> on the landing, looking up and down the well!
> The doctor will come up to us too for the last
> time there, my friend in motley. The nurse will
> look in at the curtains, and you take no notice.
> . . . Your comedy and mine will have been
> played out then, and we shall be removed. . . .
> Your son will new furnish the house, or per-
> haps let it, and go into a more modern quarter.

From this Thackeray begins a philosophical discussion: "Which of the dead are most tenderly and
passionately deplored? Those who love the surviv-
ors least. . . ." Some words that pass between Mr.

Sedley and Amelia allow Thackeray to return to
generalities by way of a curious Thackerayan gam-
bit, the hypothetical action by his character. "Perhaps as he was lying awake then, his life may have
passed before him. ... Which, I wonder, brother
reader, is the better lot, to die prosperous and
famous, or poor and disappointed?" [p.234]. Of
course Thackeray chooses the latter.

Clearly, then, Mr. Sedley's death has been used
as a text for a discussion of our own. We have
watched the scene being played out, we are given
a strong sense of the physical locale (" . . . sit on
the landing, looking up and down the well!"), but
the coffin and funeral are ours. We even get a
deathbed speech — in fact two alternative ones —
but they are both ours:

> Suppose you are particularly rich and well to
> do, and say on that last day, "I am very rich.
> ... I leave my daughters with ten thousand
> pounds apiece, . . ."
>
> Or suppose, on the other hand, your swan
> sings a different sort of dirge, and you say, "I
> am a poor blighted, disappointed old fellow,
> . . ." [Pp. 235-236]

Mr. Sedley's experience, considered with its alternative, is offered to us as a model; the details of
his death are supposed for the purposes of the
discussion ("his life may have passed before him
. . ."), the discussion being implicitly more important than the particular instance. The effect of the
opening passage is indeed to make us put down
the book and go contemplate our own stairwell,

and it is this which is fundamentally opposed to dramatic involvement. *De te fabula* means that Mr. Sedley's death becomes secondary in the face of our own, and though there are generations of readers to testify that the impulse to close the book and go to the mirror is not the only one the novel creates, that these characters do have value in their own convincing vitality, still that impulse is a major element in a vast rhetorical paradox.

Vanity Fair as Satire

Satire seeks to maximize the ridiculousness of its object of attack — presumably vanity in this case, which Thackeray generalizes to include nearly all error. This concept helps us understand the power of much of Thackeray's work which from a dramatic perspective appears only muddled and self-destructive. Whereas dramatic action seeks to create a concern for certain characters and potentialities of action and against others, a typical action in *Vanity Fair* allows no such opposition, but works to the ridicule of all parties and all possible actions. For instance, here is Mrs. Blenkinsop, Amelia's housekeeper, comforting Amelia in her grief at Jos's desertion of Becky [*VF* 6: 1:90]:

> "Don't take on, Miss. I didn't like to tell you. But none of us in the house have liked her except at first. I sor her with my own eyes reading your Ma's letters. Pinner says she's always about your trinket box and drawers, and everybody's drawers, and she's sure put your white ribbing into her box."

"I gave it her, I gave it her," Amelia said.
But this did not alter Mrs. Blenkinsop's opinion of Miss Sharp. "I don't trust them gover-
nesses, Pinner," she remarked to the maid.
"They give themselves the hairs and hupstarts
of ladies, and their wages is no better than you
nor me."

The reader who seeks a dramatic orientation finds
none to be had. Mrs. B's exposure does not save
Becky, since her charges are left mainly unan-
swered; it only destroys any attempts we might
make to disapprove of Becky as opposed to anyone
else. Examples of this are without number: When
Mr. Crump, the apothecary, saves Miss Crawley
from the killing care of Mrs. Bute Crawley, the
narrator takes care to relate Dr. Squills' earlier
advice to him — "Get her up, Clump; get her out:
or I wouldn't give many weeks' purchase for your
200 a year" [*VF* 19; 1:288]; when Horrocks, Sir
Pitt's mistress, receives her just punishment, that
punishment becomes the triumph of a more in-
sidious form of vice — Mrs. Bute's [*VF* 39;
2:268ff.]. In the first case, Thackeray lets an apparently good deed be done, then exposes its base
motives. In the second, he creates dramatic desires
(that Horrocks not be allowed to succeed in in-
heriting the Crawley estate) and shows that their
satisfaction is unsatisfying. The rhetorical process
expects us to try to read this book like a dramatic
action, so that our failure to maintain that simple
assignment of sympathies will raise questions about
the grounds for those sympathies in general.

Often Thackeray's deployment of data is aimed at inducing us to judge too simply, so that he may confront us with the dubious methods by which such judgments are made. In chapter 2, when we are attempting to characterize the mysterious Miss Sharp, we are told that Miss Pinkerton, in her innocence, mistook Becky for an ingenue and gave her a doll, which she had confiscated from a Miss Swindle, who was caught nursing it [1:77ff.]. Becky took the doll home and made a caricature of Miss Pinkerton with it. How do we interpret this? The doll is the gift of a fool and a hypocrite, and Becky's treatment of it seems to reflect a true perception of the moral spirit in which it was given. In the battle between the satirist and the hypocrite, our alliances are clear. But we next learn that after Becky's next trip to Chiswick she set up a second doll as Jemima, the innocent. Thackeray makes his point: "Though that honest creature had given her [Becky] jelly and cake enough for three children, and a seven-shilling piece at parting, the girl's sense of ridicule was far stronger than her gratitude, and she sacrificed Miss Jemmy quite as ruthlessly as her sister" [18-19]. It seems that Miss Pinkerton is punished, but not for her sins. The extent to which Thackeray prohibits one-dimensional dramatic situations, where a single consistent dramatic sympathy can encompass motivation, act, and consequence, can be appreciated when we recognize the power of the single exception to this rule. Raggles, the faithful servant to Miss Crawley, is ruined by Rawdon and Becky's living on nothing a year [chap. 37]; their domestic economy is based

proposing the match, and George for refusing it.
What this means for Miss Swartz's dramatic role
is confusion. If we assume that Thackeray seeks
to maximize the absurdity and viciousness of
George and his father, Miss Swartz becomes a
paradox — Mr. O's vice appears vicious insofar as
we see her as an unfit wife for an English gentleman, and George's vice is proportional to our perception of her as a fully valuable human being.
Used in this way, Miss Swartz gives us no sure
evidence with which to construct Thackeray's
opinions about black people — a fact that is made
more interesting when we realize that Thackeray
had a strong and undisguised opinion on the subject.[9]

The difference between Thackeray's satiric
methods and those of drama can be clarified if we
compare the employment of Swartz in this scene
with Richardson's use of Soames in *Clarissa*. Both
are unwanted suitors who appear at a critical
moment to force the hero into a necessary line of
action. But Soames clarifies and strengthens the
dramatic commitment, while Swartz muddles it.
Soames represents the final, intolerable injustice
to Clarissa by her parents, and a sexual fate more
terrible than the threat of Lovelace; rape is less
dishonorable than prostitution. His presence com-
bines with other facts to make her going necessary,
yet morally faultless, thus maintaining the tragic

[9] Cf. *Virg.* 20; 12:248—Thackeray on the subject of woman's irra-
tional love for man. "What (mental) negroes do they not cherish?
What (moral) hunchbacks do they not adore? What lepers, what
idiots," etc.

structure whereby her virtue leads her unavoidably to her doom. Swartz helps force George to marry Amelia, but for all the wrong reasons, and of course dramatically he should not be forced at all. In the moment of triumph for youthful love over parental, social, and economic forces, Thackeray reminds us of the sources of George's grand gesture in vanity, stubbornness, snobbery, and a romantic self-image. Richardson underlines our dramatic alliances at a critical moment, and Thackeray destroys them.

To ask, should George marry Miss Swartz or not, is to ask a question *Vanity Fair* cannot answer; no more can Swift answer us if we ask, what size do you want people to be, then? Satire, unlike apologue, does not imply a corresponding affirmative with its every negative. Thackeray mocks those who attempt to rise in the social system, and those who say they do not care to. He mocks the emptiness of high society, and mocks Becky when her ambitions sink so low as to be content with bohemianism [*VF* 64]. He mocks high society for admitting Becky into itself, mocks Becky for valuing the recognition, and mocks Mrs. Bute for thinking Becky unworthy of the honor [*VF* 48; 3:25]. Does Thackeray despise the *mariage de convenance*? Hear him judging *Vanity Fair*'s first love match: "Are we to expect a heavy dragoon with strong desires and small brains, who had never controlled a passion in his life, to become prudent all of a sudden, and to refuse to pay any price for an indulgence to which he had a mind?" [16; 1:233]. May we conclude that if Rawdon had valued his promised inheritance above Becky, Thackeray would have approved? Suddenly prudence has become a good word, it seems.

The terms of our discussion apparently do not fit satire. The error seems to be in assuming that the satirist must consider all possibilities before passing judgment; nothing could be further from the truth. The satirist, unlike the apologist, includes in his vision only what aids his argument. *Vanity Fair* suggests that all men are "vain" (that is, consumed by the pursuit of empty, worldly ambitions — using the word in its scriptural sense) by including only vain men. *Rasselas*, on the other hand, is obliged to consider all varieties of human occupation if its conclusion about human occupation in general is to be sound. For instance, the question, should George marry Miss Swartz or not, is unanswerable because in the satiric context the urge to marry will be motivated by greed and the urge not to will be motivated by pride. Similarly with rising in the social scale: those who seek social prominence will do so for the meanest of reasons, and those who profess not to care will be lying. *Vanity Fair* is, like most satires, premised on a tautology: only data will be included which are typical of Vanity Fair. In Vanity Fair, everyone is in pursuit of *vanitas*. That Vanity Fair resembles Victorian England is logically irrelevant. But to come round again to our central idea: this technique only seems paradoxical when we approach it with expectations of a consistency of argument or dramatic structure. Consider the Rawdon-Becky match: to marry for money is wrong; to marry with thoughtless self-indulgence is also wrong. The only

reason we might be perplexed by Thackeray's judgment of Rawdon here is that we erroneously are
reading in pursuit of a dramatic commitment —
that is, looking for a kind of marriage that is
successful, so that we can read with expectations
of a happy ending — or in pursuit of a generalized
argument, with conclusion — "therefore one should
marry in such and such a way." *Vanity Fair*, and
satire in general, has no provisions for happy end-
ings and no responsibility for logical argument. But
the point is that, unlike most satires, *Vanity Fair*
looks very much like a dramatic action, and in fact
encourages us to make that reading error, and bases
much of its rhetorical effect on the supposition that
the reader will make it.

In these terms we can deal with one of the most
troublesome critical questions about the book: Is
Becky the heroine, or not?[10] The argument that
she is says this: In a world without heroes, where
virtue is inevitably revealed as vice with a socially
acceptable face, where the choice is between greater
and lesser, or more and less skilled, villains, Becky's
wit, skill and *élan* win our sympathies, by everyone
else's default. Furthermore, Thackeray emphasizes
the ambiguity of her guilt by rendering suspect the
sources of the evidence against her; from Chiswick,
where her evil character comes from a hypocrite

[10] Though Becky's popularity may be waning, at one time it was
so fashionable to describe her as the heroine of the novel that John
Tilford felt it necessary to collect the explicit evidence of her evil
nature and present it in an attempt to modify that view. Cf. "The
Degradation of Becky Sharp," *South Atlantic Quarterly* 58 (1959);
603-608. Tilford includes a short bibliography of critical arguments
for Becky's heroic stature.

who hates Becky because Becky sees through her, to the Sedleys', where servants hate her for Amelia's attention to her, and so on until the climax of ambiguity in the Lord Steyne scene [*VF* 53], we are unsure of her purposes and responsibilities. Thackeray seems to be arguing that guilt is a purely relative thing, depending on one's social standing and whether one gets caught or not, and that moral condemnation is the act of the self-righteous and hypocritical.

We might note first that, according to Thackeray's letters and early writing, which we will examine in detail in chapter 2, if he did write a morally relativistic novel in *Vanity Fair*, it was in his own terms an egregious error. His aims, by all evidence, remain throughout his career absolutely moral. When he says he is trying to "make a set of people living without God in the world," there is no indication that his lesson is that, since we are without God, the best we can attain is a vivacious worldliness. Again, the argument seems to mistake a satire for an apologue; it presumes that *Vanity Fair* is obliged to consider man in all his ways, so that we are justified in accepting the most attractive as our model. But Thackeray is explicit about the sides of life that do not fit into *Vanity Fair*; his famous veil is drawn over all scenes of honest emotion, grief, love, or religious faith [*VF* 50; 3:53, for example], as well as hints of vice dark enough to bring out in us an uncontrollably negative response [cf. *VF* 19; 1:281-282]. There may be no life better than Becky's in Vanity Fair, but one can always leave, as later novels make explicit. The relativist argument finally comes down to the claim that, if all elements of a set share a characteristic, then for that set that characteristic no longer serves to characterize. Specifically, if all people are vicious, the concept of vice atrophies. The generalization is perhaps true in fields other than the moral, but there it is clearly not true. The argument that, since all men are guilty, the concept of guilt is meaningless, certainly would puzzle any orthodox Christian, since his religion is based on another premise. The model of Christ presumably remains.[11]

What, then, of the ambiguity Thackeray seems to work to cast over Becky's guilt? Again the error seems to be in assuming that we are somehow forced to choose preferences here. That Becky's crimes are exposed by witnesses with mean motives need not win for those crimes any extenuation. Becky is guilty, and those who persecute her are also guilty. Thackeray expects vice to inspire moral repugnance, and a world completely vicious to inspire complete repugnance. And so with the Lord Steyne scene. Thackeray asks, "What had happened? Was she guilty or not? She said not; but

---

[11] It is interesting to note that Thackeray denies to Swift the benefit of this insight into the nature of satire. In his character of Swift in the lectures on "The English Humorists," Thackeray damns *Gulliver's Travels*, and particularly book 4, as morally repugnant and leading only to the reader's despair instead of his instruction [*Works* 36:178ff.]. Thackeray's criticisms are, of course, precisely those leveled at him by a troubled Victorian public. (Compare Thackeray's remarks, p. 179, on "the fatal rocks toward which [Swift's] logic desperately drifted," with Samuel Phillips' comments on the conclusion of Thackeray's cynicism in a monstrous atheism, in Tillotson and Hawes, eds., *Thackeray, The Critical Heritage* [New York: Barnes and Noble, 1968], p. 153.) Thackeray's violent denunciation of Swift as merely destructive is largely self-defense; he is determined, throughout his career after the publication of *Vanity Fair*, to deny the hopelessness readers found in his works.

who could tell what was the truth which came from those lips; or if that corrupt heart was in this case pure?" [3:115]. But he does not mean that she may have been innocent, but only that she may not have been guilty of the physical act of adultery. This does not mean that the moral issues are not clear. We have no doubts as to the moral character of her aims or the ruthlessness of her methods, so the question of her purity here can be only a technicality. Her efforts in Lord Steyne's direction have been fundamentally prostitution always, and the indefiniteness of the line between "guilt" and "purity" is only a reflection of the fact that in Vanity Fair the difference between a worthy interest in your husband's advancement and prostitution is, again, the difference between success or failure.

Becky is not a heroine, but a satiric vehicle; like Gulliver, whose large size is exactly the right irritant to goad the Lilliputians into parading their grandiose self-images, she is exactly the right item to panic every member of Vanity Fair into a display of the form of vanity he chooses to pursue. But to suggest that Becky is heroine because she is the best of the puppets is to suggest that Gulliver is best for being the biggest of the Lilliputians. Both are finally the biggest of fools.

The structure of satire does not necessitate her status as heroine, then. But what if we grant her that role and attempt to trace out the dynamics of her dramatic situation? What are our wishes for her as heroine? What courses of action do we fear and desire? We quickly realize that she is not describable that way. If we wish social success for her, we are discouraged by repeated reminders like the following: In her dark history after Rawdon's departure and before Pumpernickel [*VF* 64], she is threatened by poverty, loneliness, and disrespect from sexually threatening male companions with cleaned gloves, when light shines from above. She is taken up by the Eagles, a genteel family.

> Becky was very respectable and orderly at first, but the life of humdrum virtue grew utterly tedious to her before long. . . . Becky was dying of weariness, when, luckily for her, young Mr. Eagles came from Cambridge, and his mother, seeing the impression which her young friend made upon him, straightway gave Becky warning. [3:294-295]

That puts to rout any dramatic expectations we may have had. Take any important event in her history, and ask whether rhetorically we are to desire it or not — the marriage with Jos, or with Rawdon, or with Sir Pitt. We do not know; dramatic expectations just do not exist for these things. We can hypothesize for her neither success nor stability.[12] For this reason, however fond of

---

[12] In this sense, our last view of Becky is a dramatic illusion. Dobbin and Amelia see her manning a booth in Vanity Fair, apparently happy and accepted by respectable society. But that is a necessary reminder of society's lack of values as Dobbin and Amelia leave it, much like the roar and dust that surround Arthur and Little Dorrit at the end of Dickens's novel. In terms of their departure, that final view is correct, but in terms of Becky's character, such an end cannot be. Happiness, security, stability cannot be achieved by her in polite society; Thackeray has violated character to make a powerful last image, and that Becky can withstand such violation is another indication of the protean character she shares with Gulliver.

Becky some of us may be, she cannot be a heroine, and for this reason also Amelia, however much we may dislike her, must be one — she is so recognizably at the center of a dramatic structure of definably good and bad plot developments.

The Structure of Self-Refutation

So far, we have described in *Vanity Fair* the framework of a conventional romantic drama, with Amelia at its center; a narrator who claims he is making an apologue, who insists on disrupting the drama to turn to generalities or to us; and a satire, with Becky at its center. Why are they all in the same book? It is, after all, Sacks' central point that the three narrative forms are inviolate and cannot be combined, any more than a sentence can be declarative and interrogative at the same time. We must either reject Sacks' argument in its fundamentals (which we are not prepared to do), or we must describe the uniqueness of *Vanity Fair* which justifies our describing it as a formal impossibility. To do this, let us return to the grounds for our rejection of the relativist view of *Vanity Fair*. It was then said that a satire, unlike an apologue, is not responsible for a complete survey of all varieties of experience relevant to its theme. Therefore, we may not conclude from the evidence of *Vanity Fair* that, since all men in the novel pursue vanity, all men pursue vanity. There is an unspecified alternative, presumably the one Thackeray keeps behind the veil. And he tells us in a letter his plans for that alternative:

What I want is to make a set of people living
without God in the world. . . . Dobbin and poor
Briggs are the only two people with real humility as yet. Amelia's is to come, when her
scoundrel of a husband is well dead with a ball
in his odious bowels; when she has had suffering, a child, and religion — but she has at
present a quality above most people whizz:
LOVE — by which she shall be saved. Save me,
save me too O my God and Father, cleanse
my heart and teach me my duty. [*Letters*
2:309]

The intensity of the conclusion shows how absolutely he trusted in a moral alternative to *Vanity
Fair*, and his method for presenting it is a recognizably familiar one — it is the conventional completion of Amelia's dramatic action. Like Jane Austen's Emma, Amelia is flawed, but fundamentally
good enough to justify efforts to save her, and the
difficulties ahead of her will methodically correct
those flaws. She will be purged of pride by poverty,
purged of selfishness by love for her child, purged
of worldliness by religion. At the time this letter
was written (after the completion of chapter 25),
Thackeray is intending that Amelia march forth
when the debacle of Becky's entrance into Vanity
Fair is complete, successfully conclude the Victorian novel she has begun, and retire, a compelling
moral lesson. But if this is Thackeray's plan, how
different is his achievement! The new Amelia is
fundamentally unchanged. Poverty has only inten-
sified her pleasure in her own self-sacrifice, her child

only allows her to perpetuate the vicarious self-indulgence her husband provided for her, and her religion is only the apotheosis of her self-deception —for instance: "She must give him [little Georgy] up: and then — and then she would go to George: and they would watch over the child, and wait for him until he came to them in Heaven" [*VF* 50; 3:50].

Amelia's novel somehow fails to come off, though it goes through the motions of a successful conclusion. We cannot seriously believe that behind Thackeray's curtain her prayers are anything but vanity in a pious guise. The distinction between Vanity Fair and the implied Other turns out to be mainly illusory.

And a look at the most general structural shape of *Vanity Fair* shows that the histories of the two girls are not followed simultaneously, but that Amelia is kept waiting in the wings as a potential moral response to the complete cynicism of Becky's world; when the lesson of Becky's experience is complete ("All her lies and schemes, all her selfishness and her wiles, all her wit and genius had come to this bankruptcy" [*VF* 53; 3:115]), Amelia comes forward as an alternative, and fails. The structure of the book is tripartite, and has a definite rhetorical effect. Part 1, chapters 1-32, establishes the character of the two girls and follows them until the conclusion of the war, at which point their histories diverge. Part 2 follows Becky's assault on high society, while Amelia is largely out of sight in her role as heroic impoverished widow. Part 2 ends with the Lord Steyne scene, and subsequently

Becky remains largely invisible while the moral character of Amelia's alternative is pursued and found disappointing. This is surely a more helpful view of our two heroines' interaction than one of two opposing moralities relativistically and simultaneously considered. And we might note that, though Thackeray can laugh at Amelia in Part 1 and be quite ruthless with her in Part 3, in Part 2 he goes some way toward recreating for her a heroic status. The romantic rhetoric surrounding her in her brief appearances as potential moral alternative to Becky in this middle section is largely uncompromised by irony. Amelia, starving virtuously in her humble cot, is every Victorian novel-reader's answer to the troublesome questions Becky's history raises; she is everyone's hope for the triumph of virtue, love, self-denial — and we can surely add clarity of dramatic commitment, and artistic coherence and closure. Because Amelia's attractiveness in contrast to Becky is not only a moral one, but an artistic one also. She offers us the hope of, along with the preservation of clear moral absolutes, a sure and satisfying relationship to the text. Again hypothesizing the Victorian reader, we may assume, as we have been doing, that the satiric form frustrates habitual dramatic techniques of reading, and that Amelia holds out hope that these techniques will finally work — we will once again have people and events we can involve ourselves with and against. Thackeray allows the conventional shape of the events to complete itself, but reinterprets those events to the destruction of any simple dramatic reading of them, as we noticed in detail with the Dobbin-Cuff episode.

We can now suggest a way the three narrative forms we have been noticing in *Vanity Fair* can interact to a thematic purpose. Becky's history is a satire. Amelia is at the center of a conventional romantic novel which is offered as the artistic alternative to the satiric vision, and which fails. The narrator allows the surface of that novel to remain intact, but uses its presence as a text for an aesthetic discussion that leads to an apologic truth: that, given the nature of man, life cannot be a successful novel. The principles by which we read novels are realistically simplistic and foolish; expectations of artistically satisfying form in the real world must prove specious. And, ultimately, a more correct use of fiction than sympathetic involvement must be found.

This scheme helps us solve some critical problems. It explains why *Vanity Fair* paradoxically uses the techniques of apologue, yet proves dramatically compelling: because Thackeray, to make his rhetorical point emphatic — that the drama is not working out satisfactorily — must involve us intensely in that drama, while keeping us critically objective enough to consider the implications of that failure. We must recognize Amelia's failure as a heroine, but we must recognize that she is one, and even wish her success as one, if her failure is to be frustrating and disappointing. Amelia's history is a statement about the failure of dramatic art in the real world, made compelling through the experiencing of that failure.

The scheme also helps explain why the final
effect of *Vanity Fair* seems more morally relativistic than either Thackeray's own morality would
lead us to expect or the satiric form alone would
account for. Thackeray rejects his own moral alternative — which has something like the effect of
a preacher admitting that, though all men are
sinners, corrupt and worldly, God is too.

The narrator uses Amelia's novel as the text for
a dissertation on the novel, the grounds for our
involvement in it and the proper use of it, its
relevance to the real world, and similar issues. It
is literary criticism and the object of that criticism.
The following chapter will look backward to
Thackeray's earlier essays and fictional experiments, to determine the grounds for Thackeray's
rejection of Amelia's novel. The later chapters will
examine his later novels, seeking to determine what
sort of narrative form, and what sort of relationship
between reader and text, Thackeray defines as the
proper ones after his rejection of those implicit in
his treatment of Amelia's history.

2: The Fiction that Is False: Criticism and the Early Experiments

What Is a "Novel"?

Since Thackeray's thinking about his art is always in terms of a straw man that he calls the novel, we must try to reconstruct that archetype to understand better what he means when he says he is writing something else. Everyone comes to his own definition inductively, generalizing to encompass all examples he has met; Thackeray's letters tell us that the evidence for his induction is quite different from our's. The novels he reads, few of us have ever heard of. We may have read Bulwer's *Pelham* or *Devereux,* but who can boast of knowing Susan Edmonstone Ferrier's *Destiny,* John Galt's *Stanley Buxton,* or Mrs. Gore's *The Fair of Mayfair?*[1] Shocking to contemplate are the consequences of a novelistic aesthetic that has to accommodate such works within it.

---

[1] Thackeray's letters mention his early novel reading on pp. 1:98, 105, 158, 187, 198, 203, 213, 224, 225, and 228.

When Thackeray refers to "a novel," it is always that genre's lowest common denominator; it is G. P. R. James or worse. It is the novel in all the ways that made "novel" still a pejorative term in the middle 1800s.[2] It is the novel of the 1830s and 1840s; and this is a surprise in the light of Thackeray's career. He is a student of the eighteenth century (as evidenced by his lectures on the English Humorists, *Henry Esmond, The Virginians,* and his lifelong plans for a history of Queen Anne's reign) in politics, in manners, in morals — in everything, it would appear, but narrative form. In considering the potentialities of the novel, he apparently sees no further than his own decades. The novel is heroic romance — or it is something else Thackeray himself might be attempting, of entirely unproven value. His evident admiration for Fielding is no contradiction here: he admires Fielding as a moralist, not as a structuralist; more obvious models for Thackeray's formal experiments — Swift and Sterne — are damned in moral terms for the narrative devices Thackeray seems most clearly to have learned from them.[3]

Though we can see rhetorical reasons for Thackeray's pretense of his art being without precedent, his insecurity about doing something that is not heroic romance seems too central to his artistic dilemma to be reduced to the status of a rhetorical

[2] Cf. Stang, *Theory of the Novel in England.* The term is a pejorative one for Thackeray: when he refers to himself and his comrades honorably, he calls them "humorists"; when he refers to them deprecatingly, he calls them "novelists."

[3] For Swift, see chap. 1, n. 11; for Sterne, see "The English Humorists," 26:367-368.

pose. As we will attempt to show, Thackeray's
search for the validity of his own fiction is based
on a truism: that heroic romance is of ignoble but
absolutely sure value, whereas what he is doing,
by being more honest, may be only fiction without
even fiction's value.

When Pendennis' novel, *Walter Lorraine*, is
talked about in the later novels, Thackeray hints
of vapid romance, awkward plot mechanics, unnatural sentiments, and all the other features of pulp
fiction that we think of Thackeray as revolting
against. Clive Newcome says of it, "It's capital . . .
I say, that part you know where Walter runs away
with Neæra, and the General can't pursue them,
though he has got the post-chaise at the door,
because Tim O'Toole has hidden his wooden leg!
By Jove, it's capital! — All the funny part. — I
don't like the sentimental stuff, and suicide and
that" [*Newc.* 4; 7:62]. And though we know the
advantages to Thackeray's parodic methods of representing contemporary fiction at its worst, yet
his portrayal of Pendennis as exactly the sort of
writer he himself is not means more than simple
irony. Thackeray loves these novels, and almost
for their very badness. In a report in *Punch* on "A
Brighton Night Entertainment" [Oct. 18, 1845;
31:163ff.], he talks about his "taste for the second-
rate": "Second-rate novels I . . . assert to be superi-
or to the best works of fiction. They give you no
trouble to read, excite no painful emotions — you
go through them with a gentle, languid, agreeable
interest. Mr. G. P. R. James' romances are perfect
in this way. The *ne plus ultra* of indolence may

be enjoyed during their perusal" [163-164]. Again, though this has the sound of irony, it is that special Thackerayan sort of irony which does not mean that he means something else. His love of pulp fiction, like most of his beliefs, is sincere, but complicated by tendencies in the opposite direction. In the Roundabout Papers, after his novels were written and in the last years of his life, he introduces himself as editor of the *Cornhill* with an essay on novel-reading. He observes a small boy reading a book and speculates about the contents:

> Do you suppose it was Livy, or the Greek grammar? No; it was a NOVEL that you were reading, you lazy, not very clean, good-for-nothing, sensible boy! It was D'Artagnan locking General Monk in a box, or almost succeeding in keeping Charles the First's head on. It was the prisoner of the Chateau d'If cutting himself out of the sack fifty feet under water (I mention the novels I like best myself — novels without love or talking, or any of that sort of nonsense, but containing plenty of fighting, escaping, robbery, and rescuing). . . . ["On a Lazy Idle Boy"; 27:4]

That neatly captures the paradox — "you . . . good-for-nothing, sensible boy!" And a problem arises: If Thackeray loves best the fiction least like his own, the fiction of most action and least possible reflection, why does he not write it?

His letters are a treacherous bog concerning such matters. His history and its consequent psychological problems are well known: the wealthy gentili-

ty of childhood, the loss of fortune through gam-
bling and bank failure, the years of desperate and
rather disreputable journalism, and the resultant
ambiguity about the status of the profession of
letters. His letters are variations on a few deprecat-
ing themes about his art: the agony of composition
[4:144]; the lack of artistic pretensions and the
pretence of a completely mercenary motive [2:13,
3:13, 4:13, 43, 146, 155]; the sense of duping the
public, and waiting for the inevitable moment of
being found out [2:625]; the admission of dullness,
and the promise that, in the very next number,
something very exciting will happen [2:630, 3:350,
4:439]; novel-writing as an unfit occupation for a
grown man — what Thackeray calls "novel-spinning" or "doing the novel business" [3: 13]; the
eternal hope of a secure appointment, in the Post
Office or elsewhere, that will free him from writing
fiction [2:427, 625]; the planned history of the days
of Queen Anne [3:299, 4:238]; and so on. Thackeray
suggests that he writes the way he does for two
reasons: because he is only in it for the money,
and because he cannot do any better. His
uniqueness is seen as a failure; his novels are not
like G. P. R. James', presumably, because he has
not James' talent. But the letters qualify that
viewpoint constantly. For example, John Motley
relates a conversation with Thackeray which hints
of higher ideals:

> "The Virginians," he [Thackeray] said, was
> devilish stupid, but at the same time most
> admirable; but that he intended to write a
> novel of the time of Henry V, which would

be his *capo d'opera*, in which the ancestors
of all his present characters . . . would be introduced. It would be a most magnificent performance, he said, and nobody would read it.
[Quoted in *Letters*, 4:85.]

Here a sense of ambivalence is strong. Thackeray's
irony, as will become evident when we confront
the narrative techniques of the novels themselves,
is not a sure directive toward definite truths beneath a lying textual surface, but rather the representation of an unsettled sense of paradoxes
operative. The irony tells us that the text is not
all of the matter, but gives us no sure indication
of what the entirety of the matter finally is; it
destroys the absolute validity of the textual surface
without offering anything absolutely valid as a
replacement. Perhaps a lengthy aside is justified
to make this clear. In "Round the Christmas Tree,"
a Roundabout Paper, Thackeray describes his
pleasure in experiencing vicariously the delights of
the Christmas season in the company of Bobby
Miseltow, a young houseguest. Thackeray and Bob
attend the pantomimes, and Thackeray enjoys
watching Bob enjoy them. Finally they go to the
zoo, and the essay ends with Bob's description of
what they saw, and Thackeray's comment:

"First I saw the white bear, then I saw the black,
Then I saw the camel with a hump on his
    back. . . .
Then I saw the elephant with his waving trunk,
Then I saw the monkeys — mercy, how unpleas-
    antly they — smelt!"

There. No one can beat that piece of wit, can
he, Bob? And so it is all over; but we had a
jolly time. ... Present my respects to the
doctor; and I hope, my boy, we may spend
another Merry Christmas next year.

Geoffrey Tillotson acutely observes that the test
of a Thackeray reader's "ripeness" is his response
to this passage.[4] The superficial realist sees only
the joke on Bob. But if Bob's wit is blind, the irony
hits equally hard at those whose eyes are open,
and who have lost a good laugh. The irony does
not point to a truth opposite to the textual surface;
rather it strikes resonant ambivalences that reso-
nate forever. And this view of Thackeray as ironist
is supported by a look at his letters, which reflect
on every page, not a single-minded innovator with
a clear sense of purpose and aesthetic principles,
but a confused man, eager for money and ashamed
of it, eager for popularity and disdainful of the
reading public, eager for fame and dubious about
the value of his art. His peculiar irony encompasses
these paradoxes; it does not resolve them.

Thackeray's reasons for loving bad novels are the
seeds for the rejection of them that *Vanity Fair*
surely is. "On a Lazy Idle Boy," from which we
quoted earlier, is an essay declaring the editorial
objective of the *Cornhill*, which is to maintain the
supremacy of fact over fiction. "Figs are sweet, but
fictions are sweeter," we are told. Even novelists
themselves "partake of novels in moderation ...

---

[4] *Thackeray the Novelist* (Cambridge: Cambridge Univ. Press, 1954),
pp. 270-271.

but mainly nourish themselves upon wholesome roast and boiled," that is, nonfiction. That fact is somehow better than fiction Thackeray probably would have agreed any day of his mature life; but we are concerned with the terms by which the sweets of fiction are hypothetically enjoyed. "O Dumas! ... I hereby offer you homage, and give thee thanks for many pleasant hours. I have read thee (being sick in bed) for thirteen hours of a happy day, and had the ladies of the house fighting for the volumes..." [27:4-5]. This reminds us of the terms of his praise of James earlier. The ideas of ease, languor, sleep, and the like recur whenever he talks about the pleasures of reading. Dumas is most fondly remembered being read at timelessly long stretches, on days of immobility of body and mind. Thackeray's letters about his youthful reading habits support this basic identification of reading with lethargy and irresponsibility. For one thing, the pace of his reading appears to be unsuited for critical perception. He commonly describes in his diary evenings that consist of a dinner, a session at the gaming tables, a novel (complete), and bed at ten, or a novel and then the theater. During his period of greatest inactivity, in France in 1832, when he was young, rich, out of school, and acutely conscious of having nothing valuable to do, his diary records about a novel a day or its equivalent [*Letters* 1:158, 187, 224, 225, 226, 234]. But this voracious reading is always being done instead of anything worthwhile; it is for him a symbol of the uselessness of his existence. "Tuesday 5. The day spent in seediness, repentance, and novel-reading"

[1:206]. "I have become latterly so disgusted with myself and art [i.e. drawing] ... that for a month past I have been lying on sofas reading novels, and never touching a pencil" [1:279]. And the perspective persists when he is writing, as well as reading, novels: "I am frivolous and futile, a long course of idleness (which novel-writing is) has wasted my intellect" [3:559].

This does not mean that novels are simply bad, but only that their usefulness is limited. In "On a Lazy Idle Boy," in his allegory about sweets vs. heartier sustenance, he lists those who properly love novels. "All people who have natural, healthy appetites, love sweets; all children, all women, all Eastern people, whose tastes are not corrupted by gluttony and strong drink ... " [p. 4-5]. The three traditional types of innocents, that is. In terms of *Vanity Fair*, we can say that the novel reader is one who is still free from the cynical insight that undercuts Amelia's drama. Thackeray's art hastens the loss of innocence, a loss that the mature narrator constantly deplores in his own case. Novels are for the young, and the beef of fact is for the old — which is only remarkable in light of Thackeray's intense dislike of old age. The equation between nonfiction and old age, and a melancholic dissatisfaction with the whole thing, are fixtures in Thackeray's thinking. "I wonder shall I have life and health to write [the history of] Queen Anne? I long to get at it in my old age, feeling that the days of novels and romances and love making are over" [4:239].[5] This tone appears in the essay "On a Lazy

[5] He says the same thing in 3:299, when he is 42 years old.

Idle Boy," when Thackeray's argument leads him
to sentiments that are hard to equate with his
professed theme — that one's diet should be fundamentally beef. He is meditating on the boy again:

> I doubt whether he will like novels when he
> is thirty years of age. He is taking too great
> a glut of them now. He is eating jelly until
> he will be sick. He will know most plots by
> the time he is twenty, so that he will never
> be surprised when the Stranger turns out to
> be the rightful earl, — when the old waterman,
> throwing off his beggarly gabardine, and clasp-
> ing Antonia to his bosom, proves himself to
> be the prince, her long-lost father. . . . He will
> get weary of sweets, as boys of private schools
> grow (or used to grow, for I have done growing
> some little time myself . . .) — as private
> school-boys used to grow tired of the pudding
> before their mutton at dinner. [p. 6]

There is a dreadful paradox here. Do not read
novels, because they are trivial; besides, they dull
your appetite for novels, and that appetite is something pure and precious. There is an exact parallel
in the Victorian paradox of sexuality: avoid sex,
because it is vicious; besides, sexual indulgence can
lead to impotence, which is the ultimate tragedy.
That little syntactic surprise about the parenthesis,
so typically Thackerayan, redoubles the pathos of
the aged guise. The speaker has not, as we first
think, "done growing," but, much more horribly,
has done growing tired — the process of encroaching
boredom has long since finished with him and left
him without appetite. Thackeray bemoans the

coming of worldliness and cynical wisdom, a process
that his fiction works to accelerate. His elegies to
his lost innocence in his last essays are as touching
as anything he ever wrote, and the reader of *Vanity
Fair* who views that novel's destruction of fictive
idealism as nothing more than a healthy maturing
of aesthetic tastes can fail to credit the pain consequent on that loss:

> "Ivanhoe" and "Quentin Durward!" Oh! for a
> half-holiday, and a quiet corner, and one of
> those books again! Those books, and perhaps
> those eyes with which we read them. ... If
> the gods would give me the desire of my heart,
> I should be able to write a story which boys
> would relish for the next dozen of centuries.
> ["De Juventute," *Roundabout Papers*: 27:91-
> 92. Written three years before his death.]

That the experience of such fiction has nothing
to do with real life, Thackeray constantly reminds
us. His favorite metaphor for indicating some distance from reality is the dramatic stage, particularly the pantomime. In all his work, dramatic
metaphors appear to remind us of the fact of the
novel in our hands, its illusion of reality as an
illusion. Thackeray reminds us, through techniques
we will examine closely in chapter 3, of our situation in the audience and the distance between the
pit and the stage, because he feels that distance
to be a profound one, separating ultimately idealism and worldly cynicism. Let us return to his
report of "A Brighton Night Entertainment," and
note that his love for what he sees rests directly
on its explicit artificiality.

> We saw, with leisure and delectation, that
> famous old melodrama, "The Warlock of the
> Glen."
> In a pasteboard cottage, on the banks of the
> Atlantic Ocean, there lived once a fisherman,
> who had a little canvas boat, in which it was
> a wonder he was never swamped, for the boat
> was not above three feet long. . . . [p. 165]

> What meant that scream? We were longing
> to know, but the gallery insisted on the reel
> over again, and the poor injured lady had to
> wait until the dance was done before she could
> explain her unfortunate case. [p. 165]

The pleasure lies in the assurance that this fiction
will never offer itself as fact. The distance between
it and reality does not compromise it. Thackeray
concludes his piece with a passage that, though
bursting with an artificially inflated rhetoric, reflects an emotion that he incorporates in his work
countless times — the discomforting return to the
real world from the world of delightful and ostentatious artifice.

> The curtain fell on this happy scene. . . . The
> ginger-beer boy went home to a virtuous fami-
> ly, that was probably looking out for him. The
> respectable family in the boxes went off in a
> fly. The little audience spread abroad, and were
> lost in the labyrinths of the city. The lamps
> of the Theater Royal were extinguished: and
> all — all was still. [p. 169]

Again, the wit does not necessarily invalidate the
emotion. "Labyrinths of the city" indeed! The

"virtuous" family of the ginger-beer boy is another nice touch. Thackeray neatly represents both the intoxicating influence of melodrama and the absurdity of trying to "read" real life in its terms. The labyrinths are much more Dickens's than Thackeray's, but he has borrowed them to make a point that is truly his own: that the melodramatic stage performance is a luxuriously comfortable thing, comfortable physically and artistically, the way reality can never be. Thackeray likes these dramas for the same reason he praises James's novels—they "excite no painful emotions," and so forth. Romance, in this definition, is art that perfectly suits all expectations, satisfies all desires, is dramatically and intellectually inert. Thackeray says elsewhere in his description of the play that two ruffians came on stage bearing swords, by which everyone knew that a fight with these swords would soon take place. It is that possibility of complete comprehension that he likes, wherein if there are swords, it is because there is to be fairly immediate use for them.

Thackeray has no hard words for G. P. R. James or *The Warlock of the Glen*, because he knows the value of what they are doing; his hard words are for his own art, which denies the reader the rewards of romance and may have no others. Thackeray dramatizes comically the necessity for his rejection of the romantic in *Rebecca and Rowena*.

Rebecca and Rowena: Romance at Home

Rebecca and Rowena is a Christmas book, a "Romance on Romance," as the subtitle says.

Thackeray embraces the unreality of the genre, declares that we have not had enough of it and that he will provide us with more, only better.

> Well-beloved novel-readers and gentle patronesses of romance, assuredly it has often occurred to every one of you, that the books we delight in have very unsatisfactory conclusions, and end quite prematurely with page three hundred and twenty of the third volume. At that epoch of the history it is well known that the hero is seldom more than thirty years old, and the heroine by consequence some seven or eight years younger: and I would ask any of you whether it is fair to suppose that people after the above age have anything worthy of note in their lives, and cease to exist as they drive away from St. George's, Hanover Square? ... A hero is much too valuable a gentleman to be put upon the retired list, in the prime and vigor of his youth. [1; 23:405-407]

The moral responsibilities of the "humorist" are here put aside:

> What, if reality be not so, gentlemen and ladies; and if, after dancing a variety of jigs and antics, and jumping in and out of endless trapdoors and windows, through life's shifting scenes, no fairy comes down to make *us* comfortable at the close of the performance? Ah! Let us give our honest novel-folks the benefit of their position, and not be envious of their good luck. [409]

Because it is central to our argument that Thackeray's parody represents a relationship to romance more complicated than simple moral denunciation, as in the case of his parodies of Bulwer-Lytton for instance, let us remind ourselves how Thackeray feels about Scott at the end of his life before we watch the consequences of those opening paragraphs:

> I have never dared to read the "Pirate," and the "Bride of Lammermoor," or "Kenilworth," from that day to this, because the finale is unhappy, and people die, and are murdered at the end. But "Ivanhoe," and "Quentin Durward"!. . . The boy-critic loves the story. Hence the kindly tie is established between writer and reader, and lasts pretty nearly for life. I meet people now who don't care for Walter Scott, or the "Arabian Nights"; I am sorry for them, unless they in their time have found *their* romancer — their charming Scheherazade. ["De Juventute"; 27:91-92]

The desire in Thackeray to be *beloved* in exactly this way is very strong; his destruction of romance is more like the sacrifice of Iphigenia than Samson's annihilation of the Philistines.

Thackeray attempts to write a continuation of *Ivanhoe*; he follows Ivanhoe and Rowena beyond the boundaries of the romantic plot, and discovers that it is very difficult to be a hero at home. This is the central point to Thackeray's habitual assertion that life goes on beyond the third volume and the happy marriage: conventional structure lies by omission. Thackeray tries to write a romance about the aspects of life romance cannot contain — much like Twain's Connecticut Yankee and his suit of armor: when considered between jousts, all its improbabilities and impracticalities become obvious. Thus Thackeray asks that Rowena cook and clean house, forces her to engage in domestic conversation, and finds her incompetent in all these skills. He must fill out her character, and he fills it out with the characteristics of the Mayfair wife. The rhetorical implication is obvious: when we look at character outside the controls of convention, we find Vanity Fair. If we are practiced readers of Thackeray we are not surprised when Ivanhoe in his travels becomes the object of attentions from the Princess of Pumpernickel [p. 467], or when we are told that Father Willibald was later canonized as St. Willibald of Bareacres [p. 410]. Formal structure, convention, style — these are obstacles to the perception of the truth, that the fictive world is Vanity Fair in disguise. After taking his characters beyond the dimensions of romance, thereby broadening the imaginative scope of the fiction, Thackeray returns to the conventional activities of romance — battles, rescues, magic, love — but the new wider perspective allows him to observe aspects of the experience romance cannot encompass — the villainy and greed of heroic field commanders, or the pitiless slaughter that brings a reputation for valor.

Thackeray's interest in the boundaries of convention and form, and the consequences of stepping out of them, is here expressed with the clarity of youthful enthusiasm. In the midst of a battle scene, things turn suddenly grisly; infants are being butchered. Thackeray interrupts the carnage:

> I just throw this off by way of description, and to show what *might* be done if I chose to indulge in this style of composition; but as in the battles which are described by [Scott], everything passes off agreeably — the people are slain, but without any unpleasant sensation to the reader . . . we will have this fighting business . . . disposed of. [p. 439]

Here Thackeray's sense of art as subtlety and deceit is strong; art makes slaughter no longer unpleasant. Thackeray is determined to "use no art at all" — or at least make us particularly conscious of the art being used. In "A Shabby Genteel Story," there are two identical sisters, a Rosencranz and Guildenstern (Bella and Linda, actually — the same joke). At one point Thackeray interrupts to note the implausibility of the convention he has just used: " 'How did the conjuror know it was our house?' thought Bella and Linda (they always thought in couples)" [2; 15:21].

Romance can no longer be written, no more than Saint Teresa can find fulfillment in Victorian England. To ask that romance take place in the kitchen is like asking that footraces be run on water as well as on the land — the new medium asserts itself and creates a new mode of going. What about those who aim higher, those novelists who try to make their art relevant for people other than children, women, and Easterners? The value of a novel "containing plenty of fighting, escaping, robbery, and rescuing" Thackeray knows, and he knows he cannot write it; the value of fiction with higher pretensions is an unsolved problem that influences everything he ever writes that is not safely parodic.

Thackeray vs. the Novel of "Sentimental Politics"

Thackeray's critical writing is so apparently foolish that we would never examine it carefully without *Vanity Fair* and the other novels taunting us, defying us to explain the excellence of the one and the badness of the other. Henry James sells his novels with the hard sell of his compelling criticism; Thackeray, outside the novels themselves, shows little understanding of and little enthusiasm for what he is doing in them, and his critical reputation probably suffered as a result. We must try to reconstruct the assumedly intelligent ideas about fiction which spark the unprepossessing criticism of the 1840s and the artistically eloquent statement that is *Vanity Fair*.

In a review of Dickens's *Cricket on the Hearth*, Thackeray, after admitting that it is a delightful book asks, is it a good book? He decides emphatically that it is not, because it is unnatural. "This tale is no more a real story than Peerybingle is a real name," he says, and he means that as a criticism. "You cannot help seeing that Carlotta is not a goddess (dancing as she does divinely) and that that is rouge, not blushes, on her cheeks."[6]

---

[6] *Thackeray's Contributions to the Morning Chronicle*, ed. Gordon Ray (Urbana: Univ. of Illinois Press, 1966), p. 88.

Rouge — Thackeray's basic metaphor for an im-
moral attempt to deceive [cf. *Phil.* 4; 1:194-195, for
example]. The moral character of what Dickens
is supposedly attempting to get away with is indi-
cated in the rhetoric: "We fancy that we see
throughout the aim of the author — to startle, to
keep on amusing his reader; to ply him with brisk
sentences, rapid conceits, dazzling pictures, adroit
interchanges of pathos and extravaganza" [pp. 88-
89]. Everything here suggests attempted deception.
Dickens tries to "keep on" amusing us, as if the
amusement persisted beyond proper limits. The
reader is being "plied with" sentences like intoxi-
cants. The text is rapid and dazzling, so that the
truth beneath the surface will not be perceived.
Dickens is even guilty of "adroitness." Later he
brands Dickens with the crime of being "dextrous"
[p. 91]. Skill is only necessary if the author seeks
to distort the image of the truth.[7]

What is it about Dickens's art which makes its
artifice bad, whereas the artifice of *The Warlock
of the Glen* makes it delightful? Thackeray has
begun in this case with the assumption that this
art offers itself as real. His prejudices on this
subject are so strong that we may mistake his
criticism for praise: "To our fancy, the dialogue
and characters of the *Cricket on the Hearth* are

[7] Thackeray reflects the same set of assumptions when he says of
Esmond in a letter, "My book just out is dreary and dull as if it
were true" (*Letters* 3:100). Literature is delightful to the extent that
it hides the dull truth. Note that Ivanhoe's reaction to Thackeray's
taking him out of the romantic world is a readiness to die (*Rebecca
and Rowena*, 7; 23:486).

no more like nature than the talk of Tityrus and
Melibeus is like the real talk of Bumpkin and Hodge
over a stile" [p. 88]. One could hardly imagine a
more rigorous realist aesthetic than one that
prefers Bumpkin to Virgil. But, as we have seen,
Thackeray would almost certainly prefer to read
Dickens than Virgil, and to read either more than
Bumpkin; the point is that Thackeray, though
defending a rigorous realist stance, as in this case,
is not a realist for aesthetic reasons, but for exclusively moral ones. It is not that Bumpkin is good
reading which causes Thackeray to side with him,
but only that Dickens and Virgil are both lies.
When Thackeray considers the possibility that
Dickens is not offering his art as real, his hostility
largely disappears. He interrupts his derogatory
remarks with this new idea: "But reconcile yourself
to this tone. Believe that the book is a Christmas
frolic — that the author is at high jinks with . . .
the public" [p. 90]. Thackeray summarizes the
"little plot, so charmingly unnatural" and advises:
"All these impossibilities, at which one might cavil
at any other time but Christmas, become perfectly
comprehensible now, and the absurdities pleasant,
almost credible" [p. 91]. He concludes we should
"take the Cricket [on the Hearth] in a Christmas
point of view" and enjoy it. The reconciliation is
not complete; he still concludes that "nature and
quiet are still better" [p. 90]. The delights of fantasy
are to be limited to feasts of misrule and other
intervals of conscious unreality and irrationality.
As long as the melodrama stays across the foot-

lights, Thackeray will delight in it; if it attempts
to step down into the audience, his moral honesty
will force him into the Bumpkin camp.

Reviewing Lever's *St. Patrick's Eve*, a novel that
attempts to treat seriously the hostility between
landlords and tenants, Thackeray considers another sort of problem that arises when a novelist
tries to do more than tell a good story. Again he
is insistent that novelists embrace the triviality of
their art.[8]

> When suddenly, out of the gilt pages of a pretty
> picture-book, a comic moralist rushes forward,
> and takes occasion to tell us that society is
> diseased, the laws unjust, ... persons who wish
> to lead an easy life are inclined to [say] ...
> I have shrewd doubts as to your competency
> to instruct upon all these points: at any event,
> I would much rather hear you on your own
> ground — amusing by means of amiable fiction,
> and instructing by kindly satire ... eschewing
> questions of politics and political economy, as
> too deep, I will not say for your comprehension,
> but for your readers'; and never, from their

---

[8] Gordon Ray, in his article *"Vanity Fair:* — A Version of the
Novelist's Responsibility," (*Transactions of the Royal Society of
Literature 25* [1950]: 87-101) argues that between the time of these
critical essays, around 1845, and *Vanity Fair* in 1847, a profound change
occurred in Thackeray's attitude toward the use of the novel for more
than entertainment, as shown by his reworking of the first draft of
Vanity Fair to include more moral didactic material. I do not find
the argument convincing, especially since the evidence of the later
novels shows that these issues, about which Thackeray is ambivalent
in the early years, remain always problems for him.

nature, to be discussed in any, the most gilded,
storybook.[9]

Though he says he objects to the novelist's lack
of qualifications, we suspect this is a red herring;
he certainly would have objected to Godwin's
novels of social reform or Cardinal Newman's religious novels. Fiction cannot discuss real social
problems for reasons more basic to fiction than
authorial ignorance. The problem lies in the fact
of fiction. "The landlords may be wickedly to blame
. . . but we had better have some other opinion than
that of the novelist to decide upon the dispute.
. . . He can exaggerate the indolence and luxury
of the [landlords], or the miseries and privations
of the [tenants], as his fancy leads him" [p. 73].
One can hardly imagine a stronger statement of
the traditional distrust of the artist as deceiver.
"He can exaggerate . . . as his fancy leads him";
and the choice we are given is one between such
stuff and statistics: "This is not the way in which
men seriously engaged and interested in the awful
question between rich and poor meet and grapple
with it. When Cobden thunders against the landlords, he flings figures and facts into their faces"
[p. 74]. And what is the error that the novelist's
indulgence of fancy is liable to lead to? Thackeray
identifies the requirements of conventional plot
resolution as one way the novelist's form compro-
mises his argument.

[9] *Thackeray's Contributions*, p. 71. Cf. p. 101 for the expression of
a similar sentiment. "Persons who wish to lead an easy life" is a typical
Thackerayan lump in the porridge, a stylistic disturbance to no
definable purpose.

At the conclusion of these tales, when the poor
hero or heroine has been bullied enough —
when poor Jack has been put off the murder
he was meditating, or poor Polly has been
rescued from the town on which she was about
to go — there somehow arrives a misty reconciliation between the poor and the rich; . . .
presages are made of happy life, happy marriage and happy children, happy beef and pud-
ding for all time to come; and the characters
make their bow, grinning, in a group, as they
do at the end of a drama when the curtain
falls. . . . This is not the way in which men
seriously . . . interested in the awful question
. . . meet and grapple with it. [p. 73]

In terms of our *Vanity Fair* discussion, Thackeray
is recognizing that in a dramatic action, as opposed
to an apologue, one's commitment is primarily to
the successful completion of the dramatic experience and only secondarily to the complete
presentation of a thematic statement. Specifically,
if one tries to treat social problems within the form
of conventional romance, the time will come when
one's thematic aims are best served by a denial
of the happy marriage, happy beef, and so on, which
the dramatic form demands, and one must choose.
Thackeray says one must choose happy beef, and
embrace one's art as an artifice, pleasantly perfect
and irrelevant to the real world. His own art, as
we shall see, does something else, but he is not sure
what status that something else has.

We have been documenting first one side and

then the other of a paradoxical attraction for
Thackeray to both sides of a dichotomy, between
the delightful and aesthetically satisfying lie that
is romance and the uncomfortable but unquestionably valuable truth that is fact.[10] The paradox
remains unresolved through all of Thackeray's life,
and thus we have resisted the temptation to call
him a realist in light of the last pages' evidence;
to do so is to forget the side of his art that is present
in every novel and which provides the tensions
pulling against his realist aesthetic that make those
novels charged with potential energy. The development that his early work leads us to expect — the
process of parody, rejection, and discovery of an
alternative aesthetic — does not describe the late
novels, because the rejection is never final, the
parodic purge never succeeds in driving out the

[10] As we have asked why, if Thackeray wants desperately to be a
romantic writer, does he not write romance, so we may ask why, if
he values dull fact so highly, does he not write it? In the last years
of his life when he became editor of the *Cornhill*, he pursued as editor
an aesthetic opposite to that pursued by Thackeray the writer during
his career. He sought to wean the public from a diet of fiction,
encouraged his writers to great brevity, and even hoped to encourage
a new kind of journalism, written by men unskilled in writing but
with expertise and personal experience in a particular field. His first
experiment was an article written by a surgeon describing the amputa-
tion of a leg. Thackeray's attempt to get away from the skilled man
of words seems particularly suggestive. This is obviously his conception
of Bumpkin's superiority to Virgil — Bumpkin On the Stile, Thackeray
might have in mind. The fact remains that, while he could dream
of giving pleasure as Scott had done, and exhort his contributors to
write briefly and factually, he chose to do neither, while exceptions
to that rule demonstrate that either was in his power (cf. *Letters* 4:160,
165, 177, note; and consider *The Rose and the Ring, Henry Esmond*,
and *Denis Duval* as examples of uncontaminated fantasy and romance,
and his travel sketches and journalistic essays as examples of factual
writing).

incubus of romance. Whereas *Vanity Fair* is a successful statement of that genre's inability to deal with the areas of experience Thackeray feels literature must confront, still the refutation must somehow be remade in each novel. Each novel wins its independence from the implicit assertions of conventional form, via two basic techniques, each the positive counterpart of his criticism of Dickens and Lever respectively: the ostentatious emphasis by the novel of its own fictionality, and the attempt to get outside the bounds of formal structure and thus free oneself from the demands of dramatic form. The two techniques perpetuate the paradox; one seeks to find value in fiction in terms of its fictionality, while the other seeks to escape the consequences of that fact. Thus, while his criticism calls for a clean segregation between art and fact, his own art represents a kind of apotheosis of the problem when the two are confused.

An Historical Digression

A survey of Victorian reading habits proves the grounds for Thackeray's criticism of Dickens and Lever to be wholly valid. Victorian writers combined a determination to use the phenomenally popular form of the conventional romance to package any thematic material and any didactic purpose, with a general failure to comprehend the assertions implicit in the nature of that form. The novel was the form in which a message was to be got to the people, just as the sixty-second television commercial is today; Cardinal Newman and Charles Kingsley preached in dramatic narratives,[11] and at least the latter was incalculably more effective through that means than he ever could have been from the pulpit.

Writers were sometimes conscious of the problems involved in using a dramatic genre to ends other than those for which it was intended, but the practical advantages were overwhelming. Tom Hughes considers the problem in the early pages of *Tom Brown at Oxford* — he apologizes for using his characters so overtly to discuss philosophical matters, and agrees with the critical dictum that the characters should tell their own story.

> What is a man to do, then, who has beliefs and writes to bring them out? You will say doubtless, dear reader, write essays, sermons, what you will, only not fiction. To which I would reply, Gladly, O dear reader, would I write essays or sermons, seeing that they take less out of one than fiction — but would you read them? You know you wouldn't. And so, if I sometimes stray into the pulpit, I do hope you won't be so ungenerous as to skip my preachings. [chap. 6]

The dual desire to teach and to be read leads to that uniquely Victorian novel structure — a theme and a love story striving for a reason to be in the

[11] Newman's *Loss and Gain* and *Callista*; Kingsley's *Alton Locke* and others.

same book together. *Coningsby, Mary Barton,* and *Tom Brown at Oxford* are all examples of the self-destruction that results from an attempt to combine a forthright confrontation of the facts of contemporary society with the vehicle of the popular romance. Of these only *Tom Brown at Oxford* uses the two opposing interests with any sense of the rhetorical power of such a disunity. Hughes uses the romance of the second half of the book to avoid the issues the first half raises. The half that centers around Tom's college career raises the question, how should a boy's education train him to lead an active and useful moral life in the world, and how successful is the English system at doing it? The progress of Tom's education is obviously leading to a void — no interests, no aims, no talents, and no occupational possibilities — when the love interest takes over the book, gives it dramatic direction and a kind of conclusion when the book ends in marriage. A useful life is not one of the alternatives before an English gentleman, but neither author, hero, nor reader is forced to recognize the fact. Instead, Tom uses romance the same way Hughes does — to fill out his life, or his book, when it has become apparent that something of more substance is not forthcoming.

Thackeray's advice, that the implicit assertions of the romantic form be recognized, is then pertinent to the work of his contemporaries. Our one serious quibble would probably be that his concept of the acceptable varieties of narrative form seems too limited; when he says "novel," he means romantic dramatic action. We would wish him to say, If a novelist wants to treat social problems, let him use a narrative form other than romantic drama; instead, he simply says that a novelist cannot write on these things, presumably because there is no other form to write a novel in.[12] This is a central problem in evaluating Thackeray's later novels, because they are so clearly experiments in search of an alternative to romantic drama, and not wholly successful ones. His is a particularly unhappy situation: a great literary talent, aware of the inadequacies of current literary forms for what he wants to do, and unable to discover a suitable alternative: thus the novels repeatedly make their statement in terms of their rejection of a romantic pattern of action which they cannot seem to do wholly without.

Thackeray's second critical principle, that the writer and reader become conscious of the fictionality of fiction, we are probably not so sympathetic with, because we do not so easily see how one can make the mistake that Thackeray fears will result from not doing so. However, not only is his fear supported by volumes of historical evidence to the effect that the fictionality of fiction is frequently lost sight of, the Victorians particularly seem to have lost sight of it. Let us take an example of

[12] Because we have used Sacks's categories to provide us with a vocabulary for Thackeray's discontent with the novel as he finds it, it is not to be assumed that Sacks shares Thackeray's simplistic view of the antagonism between dramatic narrative and argument. Sacks treats the problem with an insight and subtlety that are irrelevant to an understanding of Thackeray's conception of it.

Thackeray's literal-minded objections to fiction, suggest the defense of art we might make in reply, and note how for Victorian fiction his objection is truer than our defense. Consider an objection to the improbabilities of plot mechanics — the complaint that the chances against the novel's events occurring render the novel's experience irrelevant through its unlikelihood. Our defense would be something like this: Experience can have meaning independent of the likelihood of its occurrence. In fact, the very virtue of fiction is that it can hypothesize situations that are valuable and instructive yet which would rarely occur in real life. Thus Kafka's fiction does not assert that a man is likely to turn into a cockroach, but need only assert that, given the unlikely event, valuable observations result. Similarly, though the sequence of events in *Emma* is a lucky one, the value of the events lies not in that they do happen, but in what their happening reveals — the truths of character being "true" whether or not the events culminate in their discovery by the actors, as the truths of character revealed by Kafka's metamorphosis have always been true.

But if we look at a work like Kingsley's *Alton Locke,* we will see that its meaning is indeed dependent on its assertion that its events do happen — as if Kafka's meaning was that you are probably going to become a cockroach, and should take appropriate steps. Kingsley seeks the support of statistics; after a characterization of Chartism and the men involved in it, for example, he adds, "I entreat all those who disbelieve this apparently

prodigious assertion, to read the evidence given on
the trial of the John-Street conspirators, and judge
for themselves".[13] Yet Alton Locke's moral
response to his experience is also formed by the
rhetorical effect of the novel's coincidental structure. This becomes clear at the dramatic peak of
the novel, a scene that seriously questions the
validity of quoting court transcripts in support of
such an argument.

Locke's Chartist dreams have been destroyed.
His false love, Lillian, has married his cousin
George, pitiless exploiter of the poor and the working class. Locke contemplates suicide on Waterloo
Bridge [35; pp. 313ff.]. In the act of destroying
himself, his "spirit of mankind" is "reawakened"
by the sight of another attempted suicide. Locke
saves him and discovers that it is Jemmy Downes,
sweatshop operator and blackguard, reaping the
harvest of his selfishness. Locke takes Downes
home, where, in an astonishing scene full of "phos-
phorescent scraps of rotten fish ... and bloated
carcases of dogs" [p. 317], we find Downes' wife
and children naked and dead of fever ("The rats
had been busy already with them," we are told).
The house's water supply is the city sewer flowing
directly underneath; Downes' gin habit is a hopeless attempt to rid his mouth of the after-taste.
Downes, in hauling up a bucketful, falls into the
sewer and disappears. The children are covered
with the fine coat Downes was sewing in a desperate
attempt to feed his family. Locke catches the fever,

[13] Chap. 33 (New York: Harper and Bros., 1859), p. 297.

which brings him a divine lunacy from which he
emerges with a clear perception of God's careful
manipulation of his life's experiences to a moral
purpose. But the final touch remains to tell. Locke
returns to health to find George dead of fever and
Lillian robbed of her beauty and arrogance by the
disease. It is discovered that the fine coat Downes
was working on was George's, ordered for his wedding. Thus George is killed by his refusal to pay
a fair wage, as is everyone who touches the coat
and hopes to profit from the circumstances in which
it was made.

Locke and Kingsley draw a moral from the almost allegorical appositeness of all this: that there
is an Instrumentality shaping the design of experience. Kingsley would have it that it is God:
Thackeray would firmly remind us that it is Kingsley. An aesthetic structure is being "passed off"
as a moral one. To this sort of error the most
effective critical response is precisely Thackeray's
— to point out that it is all made up. Significantly,
the idealistic novel-reading females of his novels
make the same equation between Christian faith
and a confidence in benevolent coincidence.[14]

The Literal-Minded in Search of Truth: *A Shabby Genteel Story* and Others

Thackeray often takes this matter of the fictive
lie with Houyhnhnm-like literalness. He says in a
letter to David Masson discussing Masson's dis-

[14] Cf. chap. 5 and *Phil.* 32; 16:261. 34; 16:304. *Virg.* 21; 12:274-275,
and so on.

tinction between the idealistic art of Dickens and
the realist art of Thackeray [North British Rev.,
1851, pp. 57-89],

> [I hold] that the Art of Novels is to represent
> Nature: to convey as strongly as possible the
> sentiment of reality — in a tragedy or a poem
> or a lofty drama you aim at producing different
> emotions; ... but in a drawingroom drama a
> coat is a coat and a poker a poker; and must
> be nothing else according to my ethics, not an
> embroidered tunic, nor a great red-hot instru-
> ment like the Pantomime weapon. [*Letters*
> 2:772-773]

He concludes that Dickens's "writing has one ad-
mirable quality — it is charming — that answers
everything." The only alternative to calling a poker
a poker is a pleasing deception. One who does not
share the realistic prejudices would be quick to
argue that art can have value in other things
besides a representation of the literal surface of
reality — it can, for instance, bring order to the
meaningless chaos of experience by offering fables,
or mythic patterns by which that chaos can be
comprehended, albeit only through oversimplification it is true. But if we recognize that art seeks
to represent, not only literal reality, but the perception of reality, the oversimplification ceases to
be a lie. "Cinderella," in this context, is not a lie
about the destiny of chambermaids, but is rather
an accurate representation of a basic emotional and
moral perspective by which the literal surface of
reality is experienced. This is presumably the "false

surmise" with which Milton's swain reduces the shapeless evidence of "Lycidas" to aesthetic coherence and moral affirmation. The realist is always ready to reply that it is false surmise — Lycidas is dead, Cinderella's prince will not come — that schemata like Lycidas' immortalization within the natural cycle and Cinderella's successful marriage are not offered as literal reality is a fact easily and often lost sight of, and when taken for literal reality they can do some damage.[15]

Much of Thackeray's early fiction is devoted to exposing this error, in two ways: Thackeray's characters may expect to hear Bumpkin sound like Melibeus and be disappointed, or, more interestingly, the reader may be misled rhetorically into accepting Melibeus for Bumpkin, a great red-hot instrument passing for a real poker, and then have the basis of his error pointed out. *A Shabby Genteel Story* is a dramatization of the first method. Thackeray's language is always loaded with the language of myth and fairy tale; the events he records are typically related to the schemata of which they are individual variants, and one of the reasons he does this is to show that the myth fails to describe accurately the situation, in the same

[15] Of great, though peripheral, interest to this subject is Auerbach's discussion in *Mimesis: The Representation of Reality in Western Literature* (Garden City: Doubleday, 1957) of the principles of 12th-century romance in chap. 6, "The Knight Sets Forth," particularly pp. 117-123. Both Auerbach and Thackeray argue from an absolute theoretical dichotomy between art that imitates reality and art that seeks the realization of a self-contained aesthetic or moral ideal, a position that in both cases results in romance being seen as a monstrous tool of cultural self-justification and self-gratulation in spite of reality's evidence.

way that in *Vanity Fair* the dramatic force of the conventional structure of events fails to represent the moral character of what is going on. This, then, is almost an emblem by which Thackeray can recall in a moment the large contexts in which he is working — by relating the present dramatic moment to its mythic source, and showing the myth's failure to account for it. The pattern is repeated so often that its cadence becomes a familiar one:

That old woman, who began to look more and more like the wicked fairy of the stories, who is not invited to the Princess's Christening Feast, had this advantage over her likeness, that she was invited everywhere. [*Newc.* 41; 8:270]

We know, my dear children, from our favorite fairy story-books, how at all christenings and marriages some one is invariably disappointed, and vows vengeance; and so need not wonder that good Cousin Will should curse and rage energetically at the news of his brother's engagement with the colonial heiress. ... But nobody, including the swearer, believed much in Master Will's oaths; and this unrepentant prodigal, after a day or two, came back to the paternal house. ... He could not afford to resign his knife and fork at Castlewood table. [*Virg.* 72; 14:119]

And sometimes Thackeray addresses himself to the subject directly. On the subject of mercenary marriages, for instance:

> And so they went on in Arcadia itself, *really.*
> Not in that namby-pamby ballet and idyll
> world, where they tripped up to each other
> in rhythm, and talked hexameters; but in the
> real down-right, no-mistake country . . . where
> Daphne's mother dressed her up in ribbons and
> drove her to market, and sold her, and swapped
> her, and bartered her like any other lamb in
> the fair. [*Phil.* 9; 15:291]

A Shabby Genteel Story documents the failure of
the Cinderella myth to prove itself true in the "real
down-right, no-mistake" world. Caroline Gann, the
potential Cinderella, makes the fundamental
Thackerayan error — like all his most foolish and
most virtuous people, she thinks life is a romantic
novel. A handsome lover has come to seem almost
an inevitability, "or else what are novels made for?
Had Caroline read of Valancourt and Emily for
nothing, or gathered no good example from those
five tear-fraught volumes which describe the loves
of Miss Helen Mar and Sir William Wallace?" [5;
15:68; also pp. 25, 40, 112, 113].

The awaited Prince Charming arrives, but he is
a seducer instead of a marrier, and he tricks Caroline into running off with him by means of a sham
wedding ceremony. Here Thackeray concludes,
leaving our imaginations to supply visions of the
misery that awaits her.

It is indicative of Thackeray's opinion of his
readers' lack of sophistication that he thinks there
is a didactic purpose in all this. To write one
hundred and fifty pages to document the failure

of the Cinderella myth in real life is to presume
that that is a fresh insight, that someone needs
to be convinced. Another remarkable feature about
the tale is the sheer unpleasantness of reading
through it. It is our first example of a particularly
Thackerayan dramatic aim — self-obstruction,
frustration, and disgust. These are the aims of
parody, it is true, but parodies are usually quite
short because of the very finite value of their
achievement. *Shamela*, for instance, lasts long
enough to make its point and then ends before it
becomes tedious. But with Thackeray, these basically parodic elements are at least potentially
present on every page of novels that last for over
a thousand pages. *Philip* (though Thackeray does
not allow that these things be determined surely)
may be the longest parody in the world after *Don
Quixote*. At such lengths, parodic structures have
effects quite different from *Shamela*'s few pages.
But we can discuss this better in terms of a much
more extreme example of Thackeray's self-destructive art.

Catherine: Literature to Repulse

In the "Last Chapter" of *Catherine*, after two
hundred pages of intentional tedium, the moment
we have long been promised arrives — the murder
by Catherine of her husband John Hayes. Thackeray's treatment of that moment is a fine example
of his misleading us into making Caroline Gann's
error of mistaking art for reality. The night of the
murder is dramatized until Hayes is led upstairs,

down, down in the unfathomable waters.
["Chapter the Last"; 29:227]

This piece of mischief is followed by "Another Last
Chapter," in which Catherine and her lover meet
at night in the churchyard to settle their fates. We
will only quote the last paragraphs of a fine emotional scene.

[Max] stood still, and stared with wild eyes
starting from their sockets. . . . "Look, Cat —
the head — the head!" Then uttering a horrible
laugh, he fell down grovelling among the
stones, gibbering and writhing in a fit of epi-
lepsy.

The head of the murdered man is seen to be posted
on the top of the stake against which they were
leaning.

The wretched woman fled — she dared look
no more. And some hours afterwards, when,
alarmed by the Count's continued absence, his
confidential servant came to seek for him in
the churchyard, he was found sitting on the
flags, staring full at the head, and laughing,
and talking to it wildly, and nodding at it. He
was taken up a helpless idiot, and so lived for
years and years; clanking the chain, and
moaning under the lash, and howling through
long nights when the moon peered through the
bars of his solitary cell, and he buried his face
in the straw. [231-232]

Here the tale proper ends; the author draws a line
across the page and discusses what he has done.

and sounds of scuffling are heard. Thackeray continues in a new voice and a new type face:

Here follows a description of the THAMES AT MIDNIGHT, in a fine historical style. ... A combat on the river is described, that takes place between the crews of a tinklerman's boat and the water-bailiff's. Shouting his war-cry, "St. Mary Overy *à la rescousse!*" the water-bailiff sprung at the throat of the tinklerman captain. The crews of both vessels, as if aware that the struggle of their chiefs would decide the contest, ceased hostilities, and awaited on their respective poops the issue of the death-shock. It was not long coming. "Yield, dog!" said the water-bailiff. The tinklerman could not answer, — for his throat was grasped too tight in the iron clench of the city champion: but drawing his snickersnee, he plunged it seven times in the bailiff's chest: still the latter fell not. The death-rattle gurgled in the throat of his opponent; his arms fell heavily to his side. Foot to foot, each standing at the side of his boat, stood the two brave men, — *they were both dead!* "In the name of St. Clement Danes," said the master, "give way, my men!" and, thrusting forward his halberd (seven feet long, richly decorated with velvet and brass nails, and having the city arms, argent, a cross gules, and in the first quarter a dagger displayed of the second), he thrust the tinklerman's boat away from his own; and at once the bodies of the captains plunged down, down,

"Having indulged himself in a chapter of the very finest writing," he directs our attention to the merits of the piece: It is "perfectly stilted and unnatural," the characters speak impossibly, and, most of all, vice has been made to seem to deserve our sympathy. To demonstrate the distance between all this and the facts of the case, Thackeray then quotes at length, from the *Daily Post* of 1726, the report of the crime, the trial, and the following executions.[16] And he again discusses the effect of what he has done. In the role of editor discussing the author's work, he says,

> The "ordinary" narrative [i.e. from the newspaper] is far more emphatic than any composition which he might employ. Mr. Aram's trial, as taken by the penny-a-liners of those days, hath always interested him more than the lengthened and poetical report which an eminent novelist has given of the same. . . . We very much doubt if Milton himself could make a description of an execution half so horrible as the simple lines in the *Daily Post* of a hundred and ten years since, that now lies before us. [234-235]

The message is finally similar to that of *A Shabby Genteel Story*, but the method is different. Here, after hundreds of pages of stifling tedium, Thackeray offers us two "artful" perspectives on the deed

[16] These brutal, fascinating passages were judged to have no lasting value and are omitted from all collected editions of Thackeray's works, thereby denying Thackeray his best evidence for his didactic purpose. They are obviously essential to the successful completion of his argument.

of murder, and then faces us with the truth of the murder in its naked newspaper form, with no "art," in the sense of cunning distortion. The assumption that Thackeray makes, that the newspaper is somehow free from the distortions of style, perspective and rhetorical intent, is fundamentally a moral one; the newspaper report makes the murder sordid and repulsive, while Bulwer's novel makes crime seem somehow worthy of sympathy; consequently the newspaper must be truer. We are probably more willing to agree with him that a poker is a poker than that a murder is only a murder and that consequently any extenuation can only be rouge, to hide the ultimate fact. Thackeray interprets our eagerness to enjoy the two absurd scenes of violence morally, as an eagerness to avoid the moral truth that murders are unglamorous things, whereas it may be only impatience with Thackeray's overlong demonstration of the truth, certainly of limited value, that common life is dull. Yet finally I think we would deny even his premise that a poker is a poker. Thackeray's views on style are based on a realistic aesthetic that is simply untenable — that there is an "honest" style, a style without style, where words stand for things and things are demonstrably real. Thus "embroidered tunic" is deceit and "coat" is not, just as the newspaper account is the truth, which Bulwer's novel distorts. But, as we all know, the newspaper has its own formal and rhetorical assertions implicit in it, and "coat" is ultimately as rhetorically assertive as "tunic," only perhaps less obviously so. We might even wish to argue more subtly that there is no

solid reality to events independent of their evaluation in words — that the human act of perception
is inextricably one of evaluation — an emphasis on
characteristics judged essential, and so on. Thackeray's assumption of a possible styleless style is a
chimera, but essential to his hopes for the novel.

Catherine is attacking a particular genre of fiction. Newgate fiction, an expansion of the Newgate
Calendar's materials to novel length, was extremely
popular at the time of Catherine's appearance
(1839).[17] Thackeray specifies as representatives of
the genre he attacks Ainsworth's *Rookwood* and
Jack Sheppard, Bulwer's *Ernest Maltravers* and
Eugene Aram, and Dickens' *Oliver Twist*. The basis
for his moral indignation is not profound: it is
simply that these works make vice attractive, or
at least forgivable. Thackeray sees no moral justifi-
cation for making a whore sympathetic (Dickens's
"Bis Dadsy," as Thackeray mockingly calls her).
His objection is given no more elaborate expression
than the complaint that prostitutes and highway-
men "don't talk that way."[18] Thackeray's assertions about the moral effect of these works would
seem to be simply inaccurate, but his parody of
what he thinks is there can be very funny. In his
earlier *Novels by Eminent Hands*, he parodies
Bulwer's *Eugene Aram* by rewriting the history
of the murderer George Barnwell in Bulwer's in-

[17] A fuller discussion of the Newgate Novel may be found in Keith
Hollingsworth's *The Newgate Novel 1830-1847* (Detroit: Wayne State
Univ. Press, 1963).
[18] Much of Thackeray's discussion of Dickens' impropriety in creating Nancy is in those passages deleted from the final chapter in all
collected editions.

flated style, and defending the murder as an act in harmony with cosmic forces of Beauty and poetry. By implication, Thackeray would prefer Mr. Pumblechook's use of the tale — to terrify Pip into guilt-ridden meekness [*Great Expectations*, chaps. 15-16].

Thackeray sees the source of the illusion these books create in a perfidious style, and he sets out to dispel the illusion with its opposite. What he calls his " 'Catherine' cathartic" is a nauseating dose of hard-nosed reality, which will dramatize the dishonesty of any attempt to make vice even palatable. He tells the reader concerning the character of his players, "You ought to be made cordially to detest, scorn, loathe, abhor and abominate all people of this kidney" [3; p. 59], and in his conclusion he claims to have been successful:

The author has been pleased at the disgust which his work has excited, and has watched with benevolent carefulness the wry faces that have been made by many of the patients who have swallowed the dose.... [pp. 236-237]

[The author] humbly submits that, in his poem, no man shall mistake virtue for vice, no man shall allow a single sentiment of pity or admiration to enter his bosom for any character of the piece; it being, from beginning to end, a scene of unmixed rascality performed by persons who never deviate into good feeling ... [the author] feeling the greatest disgust for the characters he describes, and using his humble endeavour to cause the public also to hate them. [p. 238]

Thus *Catherine* is Thackeray's attempt to write precisely the literal truth of life, and his failure to achieve his ends is representative of a lifelong conflict of interest. For that it goes wrong even Thackeray privately testifies. In a letter to his mother he says,

> Catherine ... was a mistake all through — it was not made disgusting enough that is the fact, and the triumph of it would have been to make readers so horribly horrified as to cause them to give up or rather throw up the book and all of its kind, whereas you see the author had a sneaking kindness for his heroine, and did not like to make her utterly worthless.[19] [*Letters* 1:433]

But *Catherine*'s problems lie deeper than that, and the terms in which we discussed *Vanity Fair* will help us clarify what they are. As we mentioned when discussing Thackeray's restrictions on the aims of his fellow novelists, the error lies in his assumption that there is only one narrative form available — the dramatic action; in this case it leads him to assume that there are only two possible responses to a text: dramatic sympathy or dramatic repulsion — with their consequences, moral approval or rejection. His advice to the reader recognizes only two possible alternative responses: "No, my dear Madam, you and your daughters have no right to admire and sympathize with any such persons ... : you ought to be made cordially to

[19] *Barry Lyndon*, written in 1844, is probably more successful in these aims.

detest, scorn, loathe, abhor," and so forth [p. 59].
His rhetorical aim is based on the assumption
(almost surely correct in his own time) that the
reader will seek a dramatic orientation to his text;
Thackeray tells him repeatedly that those fixed
habits will mislead him here, that to seek a dramatic commitment, *even to take an interest,* is to
misread. Thus Thackeray demands that we confront the text freshly, without the security of
conventional directives to reading. This is the
meaning of "a novel without a hero" — a narrative
without sure, familiar signposts to the reader's
evaluation and involvement. But, in *Catherine* as
in *Vanity Fair*, Thackeray's narrative techniques
lead us to an orientation that is not dramatic, and
therefore neither attraction nor repulsion, but
Something Else, and that Something Else leads
him, in spite of his moral absolutism, into a subtler
insight into the nature of vice than that morality
should allow. The progress begins in blacks and
whites:

> We say, let your rogues in novels act like
> rogues, and your honest men like honest men;
> don't let us have any juggling and thimble-rig-
> ging with vice and virtue, so that, at the end
> of three volumes, the bewildered reader shall
> not know which is which; don't let us find
> ourselves kindling at the generous qualities of
> thieves, and sympathizing with the rascalities
> of noble hearts. [1; p. 39]

Strange words from the creator of Becky Sharp,
words with which all admirers of Miss Sharp will

have to come to terms. But Thackeray's own techniques destroy the purity of those distinctions. For
instance, when Hayes, a snivelling coward, falls in
love with Catherine, a vain, coarse ex-mistress,
Thackeray authenticates that experience in a way
habitual with him: "O cruel cruel pangs of love
unrequited: Mean rogues feel them as well as great
heroes. Lives there the man in Europe who has
not felt them many times? — Who has not knelt,
and fawned . . . " and so on for some time. As it
is elaborated, it is our passion, not Hayes': "Now
a sly demon creeps under your nightcap, and drops
into your ear those soft, hope-breathing, sweet
words, uttered on the well-remembered evening:
there, in the drawer of your dressing-table . . . lies
the dead flower that Lady Amelia Wilhelmina wore
in her bosom on the night of a certain ball". And
Thackeray is led to an inevitable conclusion: "No
mistake can be greater than that of fancying such
great emotions of love are only felt by virtuous
or exalted men: depend upon it, Love, like Death,
plays havoc among the *pauperum tabernas*, and
sports with rich and poor, wicked and virtuous,
alike" [1; 24-25].

He has done more than simply muddle the distinction between the vicious and the virtuous by
dwelling on the universal human heart they share;
he has made us look foolish, and by thus attacking
us with his wit he has distracted our attention from
the moral issues of rogues and honest men completely. He has characterized Hayes' love-sickness
as being as foolish as the reader's own, and thus

has rhetorically made us put down the fiction of John and Catherine Hayes and consider the dead flower in the dressing-table, just as he made us put down the not-very-intriguing death of Mr. Sedley to go and gaze at our own stairwell. Such stuff leads neither to sympathy nor disgust, but away from the dramatic situation entirely. The device becomes almost a reflex. The description of Hayes' proposal comes like this: "What passed between them? If your ladyship is anxious to know, think of that morning when Sir John himself popped the question" [p. 78]. Rhetorically, the effect is not that the equality of a cowardly clown and your ladyship has been asserted, but that your ladyship has just been degraded by a comparison with that clown. This matter of rhetorical thrust is quite a crucial one. When Thackeray finally concludes that "the only sad point to think of is, ... how dreadfully like a rascal is to an honest man" [p. 97], only the rhetorical context determines whether that is a defense of the rascal, a cut at the superficially honest reader, or a simple statement of the problems of making clearcut moral distinctions. But we are getting close to the reasons for this technique, the reasons why Thackeray could not successfully write a work that distinguishes the rogues from the honest men: because, while doing so would satisfy one half of his moral vision by condemning utterly the wicked, it would frustrate the other half, the preacher half, which must disconcert the self-righteous. By condemning Catherine and Hayes as vulgar, dishonest, cowardly villains, he must implicitly

commend the reader, who is apparently none of
those things. Thackeray's main concern, when it
comes to a choice, is always with the social and
moral level of his readership and himself, and he
is more concerned with the moral questions of
socially profitable virtue and socially acceptable
vice than with murder. So the vision of Catherine's
total moral repugnance is diluted by the suggestion
that we are little different from her, and the dramatic force of a totally negative response is replaced with that Something Else that allows more
complex critical judgments and an easy extension
from the text to ourselves. And it is interesting
to note in this context that the newspaper, which
Thackeray values so much more highly than the
"poetical report" of the artist, seems to lead
Thackeray to the same sort of use of his text.

> We very much doubt if Milton himself could
> make a description of an execution half so
> horrible as the simple lines in the *Daily Post*
> of a hundred and ten years since, that now
> lies before us . . . as bright and clean as on the
> day of publication. Think of it! it has been
> read by Belinda at her toilet, scanned at "But-
> ton's" and "Will's," sneered at by wits . . .
> — a busy race that hath long since plunged and
> vanished in the unfathomable gulf toward
> which we march so briskly.
> Where are they? "Afflavit Deus" — and they
> are gone! Hark! is not the same wind roaring
> still that shall sweep us down? and yonder
> stands the compositor at his types who shall

> put up a pretty paragraph some day to say
> how, "*Yesterday*, at his house in Grosvenor
> Square," or "at Botany Bay, universally re-
> gretted," died so-and-so. Into what profound
> moralities is the paragraph concerning Mrs.
> Catherine's burning leading us! [p. 235-236]

The obvious inconsequence of the thought process
perhaps makes his commitment to the conclusion
more striking. Even the newspaper is to be read
hypothesizing ourselves as the subject of the articles; the meditation on us is so primary in importance that the most extreme *non sequiturs* are
justifiable in getting from the text to it. The particular text becomes important only in its general
features, as an emblem of mortality. Thackeray
gives us here a demonstration of the kind of reading
his narrative style tries to teach us to do.

We have attempted to paint a picture of Thackeray falling between the two stools of an attractive
lie called the "novel," and a morally compelling
force called reality. Furthermore, we have noted
that, in his attempts to reconcile the two, his
conception of what a novel can be is limited to
conventional romantic drama. We will now look
at the techniques of the late novels and their
repeated attempts to divorce their meaning from
a conventional structure of events Thackeray
seems to feel they cannot exist without, and especially those techniques by which Thackeray hopes
to validate his work: the ostentatious declaration
of his art's own artfulness, and the attempt to
destroy his own dramatic form and thus free him-

self from the demands of art. Afterwards we will
consider to what extent Thackeray is successful
in finding a ground for his fiction more stable than
the balance of paradox.

3: The Structure of
the Narrative: Principally
The Newcomes

Preface: *Pendennis* and a Problem

We are struggling to escape a simplistic view of
Thackeray's career which an appreciation of his
"contribution" to the genre of novel seems to encourage. By that view, *Catherine* is the manifesto
of the new school — a manifesto directing the
novelist to draw things exactly as they are; *Vanity
Fair* is the irrefutable demonstration of the old
school's inability to deal with relevant issues; and
the later novels proceed to present the new aesthetic *Vanity Fair* demonstrates the need of —
Realism, where the complexity of human character
is represented, where the infinite ambiguities of
moral judgment are recognized, where the absolute
assertions of conventional dramatic structure are
escaped through a purposeful inartfulness. An historical critic naturally emphasizes this view, because he is more interested in how artists differ
from their peers and predecessors than in how they

are the same. But if we wish to describe Thackeray accurately, and especially if we want to account for the near unreadability of the late novels — such great "contributions," yet such poor reading — we must recognize that the historian has over-simplified.

Thackeray's role as truth-bringer is a high-sounding one. Here is Theodore Martin, a great appreciator of Thackeray's "contribution," writing in 1853 about it:

> Things had ceased to be called by their right names; the principles of right and wrong were becoming more and more confounded; sham sentiment, sham morality, sham heroism, were everywhere rampant; and romance-writers every day wandering farther and farther from nature and truth. ... Mr. Thackeray did his utmost to demolish this vicious state of things.[1]

Martin goes on to praise specifically Thackeray's rejection of the old system of poetic justice [pp. 179-180]. But such an attitude is utterly routed by *Philip*, the conclusion of which must be summarized to be appreciated. Philip has brought upon himself an honorable poverty by refusing to cajole the dying Lord Ringwood, who, he knows, plans to leave his fortune to Philip. Lord Ringwood in anger destroys the will and immediately dies in his carriage. An earlier will makes no mention of Philip. This problem is resolved in the novel's last pages: Woolcomb, heir to Ringwood's title, Philip's com-

---

[1] *Westminster Review*, April 1853, p. 363-388; reprinted in Tillotson and Hawes, eds., *Thackeray, The Critical Heritage*, p. 179ff.

petitor in love and fortune, is seeking to represent Whipham in Parliament. Philip throws his insignificant weight on the side of the opposition. Woolcomb is a mulatto, a miser, a wife-beater, a boor, and a coward, and will undoubtedly win through the force of his title and political inertia. On the day of the election, Philip hires a donkey cart to pull an insulting tableau of Woolcomb through town. Woolcomb appears in his carriage and attempts to ride down the procession. There is a crash; Woolcomb's carriage splits itself on the statue of the late Earl of Ringwood in the middle of the square. Inside a secret compartment in the carriage door is discovered the late Earl's will, thought to be destroyed. The old Earl had secreted it there upon taking it from his lawyer's and died before altering or destroying it. Philip's wealth is restored. Thackeray underlines the fantastic nature of all this: "And was the tawny Woolcomb the fairy who was to rescue Philip from grief, debt, and poverty? Yes. And the old postchaise of the late Lord Ringwood was the fairy chariot" [42; 16:478].

An appreciation of Thackeray as innovator will be simply baffled by *Philip*, but in *Pendennis* such an interpretation is directly refuted. *Pendennis'* famous preface appears to be exactly the realist manifesto we would expect to follow *Vanity Fair*: it is an *apologia* for an art more honest than entertaining ; an "exciting," "precise," and "elaborate" plan was laid aside when the author realized that he lacked the personal experience necessary to portray criminals as they are. Also, "to

describe a real rascal, you must make him so
horrible that he would be too hideous to show; and
unless the painter paints him fairly, . . . he has no
right to show him at all." "Society will not tolerate
the Natural in our Art," Thackeray complains, and
he warns us that this work attempts to correct that
false taste: "If truth is not always pleasant; at any
rate truth is best. . . . " We do not seem to have
progressed beyond *Catherine*'s aesthetic of an inartful, distasteful, yet morally compelling reality,
portrayed at the expense of conventional expectation and symmetry of design. But the rebellious
spirit of the preface is belied by the experience of
the novel.[2]

Pendennis is intended by Thackeray to refute
the charges of "pococurantism" unanimously
directed against him by contemporary reviewers of
Vanity Fair,[3] and by so defending himself he rejects
much of what for us represents *Vanity Fair*'s
unique value. The center of *Vanity Fair*'s value
is that it is a novel without a hero — that is, that
the absolute assertions of dramatic role and structure are not allowed to remain inviolate, but rather
are sacrificed to a more complex insight into
character and motivation. But Pendennis' matura-
tion process takes him through a period of *Vanity*

[2] Perhaps this is implicit in the precise terms of Thackeray's complaint. His defense of the Natural refers specifically to his portrayal
of Pen's near-affair with Fanny Bolton, but it is more a statement
of what he wished to do than of what he did. The preface is finally
more a profession of unwilling obedience to social dictates than
defiance.

[3] See *Thackeray, The Critical Heritage* for a survey, and Masson,
in the same volume, pp. 111-127, for an intelligent consideration of
the charges.

Fair-style cynicism and out the other side to a reaffirmation of romantic absolutes (at least absolutes of good, if not of evil); Thackeray unqualifiedly condemns him for his disbelief in heroes. Pendennis is, we may imagine, an enthusiastic modern reader of *Vanity Fair*, and Thackeray tells him sternly that he has mistaken the meaning. When Pen speaks from the depths of his cynicism, it seems a perfect summary of the "theme" of *Vanity Fair*:

> He was thinking what a mockery life was, and how men refuse happiness when they may have it; or, having it, kick it down; or barter it, with their eyes open, for a little worthless money or beggarly honor. And then the thought came, what does it matter for the little space? The lives of the best and purest of us are consumed in a vain desire, and end in a disappointment. . . . The stone covers over our hopes and our memories. Our place knows us not. [66; 6:262]

Thackeray himself has said the same words over a dozen gravestones; but now he condemns them utterly, and the refutation is in terms morally absolute and unabashedly romantic. The existence of two saints — Mrs. Pendennis and Laura — is the evidence by which Pen's cynical disbelief is routed. "I think for some of you [women] there has been no fall," Pen says after he has seen the light, and it is on exactly that sort of ideal, unearthly moral perfection that Thackeray bases Pen's new faith. Pen's contrition turns on it. " 'Our mother is an angel with God,' Pen sobbed out. . . .

'Teach me my duty. Pray for me that I may do
it — pure heart' " [70; 6:315]. And the narrator
speaks of such women in similarly uncompromising
terms of moral idealism.

> Did you ever know a person who met Fortune
> in that way [i.e. with an optimistic smile and
> resignation], whom the goddess did not regard
> kindly? Are not even bad people won by con-
> stant cheerfulness and a pure and affectionate
> heart? When the babes in the wood, in the
> ballad, looked fondly and trustfully at those
> notorious rogues whom their uncle had set to
> make away with the little folks, we all know
> how one of the rascals relented, and made away
> with the other — not having the heart to be
> cruel to so much innocence and beauty. Oh,
> happy they who have that virgin loving trust
> and sweet smiling confidence in the world, and
> fear no evil because they think none! Miss
> Laura Bell was one of these fortunate persons;
> and besides the gentle widow's little cross,
> which, as we have seen, Pen gave her, had a
> sparkling and brilliant *kohinoor* in her bosom,
> as is even more precious than that famous
> jewel; for it not only fetches a price, and is
> retained by its owner in another world where
> diamonds are stated to be of no value, but here,
> too, is of estimable worth to its possessor; is
> a talisman against evil, and lightens up the
> darkness of life. [66; 6:253]

After *Vanity Fair*, how can Thackeray say that
virgin innocence is a talisman against evil? How

can he expect to use the Babes in the Wood as
·an authoritative reference? How can he answer the
evidence about man's heart that *Vanity Fair*
amasses with "Our mother is an angel with God,"
and expect the answer to be compelling? If Pendennis' first mistake is to believe in heroes, and
his second is not to believe, what is the proper
balance of youthful idealism and disillusioned cynicism that is being recommended here? *Vanity Fair*
convincingly demonstrates the error of the first
mistake; *Pendennis* attempts to demonstrate the
error of the second, but with dubious success, since
the only two pieces of evidence Thackeray has
against nine hundred pages of worldliness and selfishness, Laura and Helen, wear their crowns of
saintliness at a distinct bias. Does a truer insight
follow these two books, the first of which seems
to be a refutation of contemporary modes, and the
second a refutation of the refutation? We will hope
to arrive at an answer by asking a smaller question:
What style can encompass a Becky and a Helen
Pendennis, a *Vanity Fair* and a *Philip,* an ironic
vision of universal viciousness and that sermon on
Laura's pure bosom, replete with delicate echoes
of Christ's parables [the "pearl of great price" of
Matt. 13:45-46]?

Narrative Structure: *The Newcomes*

Reading *The Newcomes*, one swears that part
of the book is missing — necessary information
seems to have been excluded. To reread the book
is to discover that "missing" information is present,

but presented in ways that make the reader overlook it; the materials of a coherent dramatic action
are collected between the book's covers, but out
of order, without proper dramatic emphasis, and
without the connectedness that makes dramatic
moments memorable by their place in larger structures. Thackeray is dealing with themes that are
represented by events independent of their causes
and consequences; no reader of Thackeray is left
with a strong sense of a progressive plot.

Geoffrey Tillotson says, in the beginning of his
book on Thackeray, "I do not propose to prove
that his plots, though lacking design, have the
power of making us read on to see 'what happens.'
That they have this primary and necessary source
of continuity I take for granted."[4] But these matters are not to be taken for granted; Thackeray
teaches us that "essentials" of dramatic construc-
tion like dramatic expectation and satisfaction are
not essential; not only does he not ask for that
kind of dramatic commitment from the reader, but
if we commit ourselves unasked we will be frustrat-
ed — one who reads *The Newcomes* to see "what
happens" between Clive and Ethel, the center of
sympathetic and thematic interest in the book, in
the end will be laughed at for caring and told to
finish the fantasy in whatever way suits his fancy
[chap. 80].

In fact, an understanding of Thackeray's novel
is only slightly dependent on remembering "what
happened," as it is primarily dependent on it in
a novelist like Jane Austen. In Austen, an act or

[4] *Thackeray the Novelist*, p. 22.

event has meaning in terms of its causal relationship with what precedes and follows, but Thackeray's scenes occur *in vacuo*, and can be located
only within extreme limits — a conversation
between Clive and the Colonel about Rosie must
occur after Rosie's appearance and before her
death, for instance. When the speaker is the narrator or one of Pen's permanent acquaintances, the
passage can be transferred to almost any place in
any of the Pendennis novels. If Thackeray's meaning is contained in episodes without dramatic con-
nections between them, he must be working with
concepts of character, and must be seeking moral
ends, quite different from those of the classical
dramatic novel; and the question can legitimately
be raised whether Thackeray's new aims are in any
essential way involved with or furthered by the
conventional novel format. For one example:
Emma's voice and actions can be "dated" in the
novel's chronology, at least in theory, by the degree
of moral self-awareness she shows, since the novel
follows that sequential development. Thackeray's
characters generally have no such development —
Colonel Newcome enters the stage complete and
changes not a whisker until his death — and we
may legitimately ask what the advantages are in
observing him for eight hundred pages beyond the
point when we have him pretty fully understood.

Often information we receive is fixable in the
chronology of the story, but not to be located at
any specific place in the writing out of the novel.
Lord Kew, for example, has a fairly complete history, but it comes in bits at odd times, after the

events it explains, out of chronological order and spread through hundreds of the novel's pages [8:212, 203; cf. 8:169]. It is because Pen, the narrator, is *telling* Kew's story instead of witnessing or dramatizing it, that he is able to release these items whenever he wants to, but Pen, by means of some simple devices, works to turn a very large part of his novel into past history, so that he may thus tell instead of show. If one begins reading *The Newcomes* with conventional priorities, whereby telling summarizes background information so that we can understand the important things we are about to see, one will realize somewhere in the second volume that what he thought was preliminary spade work is not clearing ground for scenes of dramatic immediacy; on the contrary, when Pen catches up to the dramatic present he leaps ahead to a dinner or other social gathering, so that he may treat the time in between as past time. The pattern is repeated numberless times: we leap forward in time, the outcome of the overlept events is discovered through impersonal media — anonymous dinner conversation, town gossip told to no one in particular, the breakfast newspaper, a letter — and Pen explains how it came about. And there is this device:

> And now, having partially explained how the Prince de Moncontour was present at Mr. Barnes Newcome's wedding, let us show how it was that Barnes' first cousin, the Earl of Kew, did not attend that ceremony [36; 8:199].

> And now we must tell how it is that Clive

Newcome, Esq., whose eyes are flashing fire
across the flowers of the table at Lord Highgate
... — now we must tell how it is that Clive
and his cousin Barnes have grown to be friends
again [48; 8:407].

The quintessential scene in this novel is a dinner,
during which Pen gives us the recent history of
everyone who is or is not there, explaining their
presence or absence. Pen recognizes this fact about
his method: "Our tale ... has passed in leisurely
scenes wherein the present tense is perforce adopted; the writer acting as chorus to the drama, and
occasionally explaining ... how it happens that the
performers are in such and such a posture" [25;
7:408].

The scenes we see are "leisurely" in that they
are without any agitating dramatic interest or
dramatic thrust in any direction; they neither move
nor move us. They are scenes of breakfast or dinner,
at which the vital events of "plot" are remarked
upon. If we were to summarize the important plot
elements of volume 1 — Clive's proud vanity and
prodigality, which must be curbed; his love for
Ethel, and the unjust barriers of profession, social
class, and fortune which separate them; Colonel
Newcome's vain hopes for reliving his youth vicariously through his son, and the disappointment
of those hopes — we would find these themes
perfunctorily set down in one- or two-page essays
by Pen and rather ignored, while hundreds of pages
are filled with matter that our training in dramatic
priorities tells us is less important. Clive's defects

of character are set down in a paragraph after a complete failure to present them dramatically, and they never become a causative factor in the working out of the action [18; 7:293-294]. The Colonel's expectations and disappointments get a passage [21; 7:331ff.]. Clive's unrequited love for Ethel is so manifestly meant to serve as a love interest, yet is so manifestly undocumented, that we are unsure if we are to think it real, until we get this typically Thackerayan explanation in the third volume:

> Our young man was changed. During the last fifteen or twenty months the malady [of love] had been increasing on him, of which we have not chosen to describe at length the stages; knowing very well that the reader (the male reader at least) does not care a fig about other people's sentimental perplexities, and is not wrapped up heart and soul in Clive's affairs like his father [51; 9:4].

In other words, the novel has been going on, Pen assures us, but behind our back, Pen feeling that we would be more interested in something else.

This feeling that the central action of the novel is going on beyond our vision is heightened by Pen's relationship to his material; he is *told* the story much of the time. Thus events are presented, not in the chronology of their occurrence, but as he learns of them, as in the following: "Nearly three years had elapsed since the good Colonel's departure for India, and during this time certain changes had occurred in the lives of the principal actors and the writer of this history. ... The chronicler of these memoirs was a bachelor no longer. My wife and I had spent the winter in Rome." Upon returning, they seek Clive at a friend's: "Had we not heard? He had become a rich man, a man of fashion. . . . [His art] was improving every day, when this abominable bank came in the way, and stopped him. What bank? I did not know the new Indian bank of which the Colonel was a director?" [48; 8:400-401]. The novel is overtly *compiled* from evidence gathered over many years and in many countries, but the compilation is not yet complete; that is, Pen has brought all the relevant information together in his mind, but has not yet given it order, and as he writes he lets his memory pick its way through it. Thus we must complete the process of compilation − collecting the pieces of Lord Kew's history, for instance. This is the third and finally characteristic chronology of *The New-comes* − above the dramatic chronology of events, above the chronology of Pen's learning the story, there is the chronology of ideas suggesting others in Pen's casual and associative memory. Let us try to follow the tortuous path of association and watch how Pen seems to stumble onto dramatic material. News comes to Pen's group that Barnes Newcome, attempting to win sympathy and support in the upcoming parliamentary elections, is going to give a lecture at the Newcome Athenaeum on "The Poetry of Womanhood and the Affections" [65]. Warrington suggests they attend the lecture as hecklers. Pages later, a circuitous path has led us to the Athenaeum on that evening. In London, Pen and the Colonel have been arguing about

Barnes and the Colonel's lack of charity toward
him. The sequence of ideas goes like this (my
words):

> Some people encouraged the Colonel in his
> vindictiveness. Warrington, for instance, was
> so hostile to Barnes, he attended Barnes' lec-
> ture and made mock. Clive and the Colonel
> were also in Newcome at that time. It was said
> they were there to visit the Colonel's old nurse,
> Mrs. Mason. She was so old, she confused the
> Colonel and Clive in her mind. "A lady"
> thought she was wandering when she spoke
> of a visit from her boy. Mason's attendant told
> Ethel that Clive and the Colonel actually had
> been there. Ethel was quite upset — the attend-
> ant told the Colonel when they came to visit.
> "Did she often come to visit Mrs. Mason?" the
> Colonel asked, not mentioning that he had met
> her at the door moments before. Ethel had
> been talking to Dr. Harris at the time. She
> went to greet the Colonel and was snubbed.
> The Colonel did not mention it to Clive; but
> surely Dr. Harris mentioned it to the members
> of the club as they assembled to discuss
> Barnes' lecture afterwards.

A description of the scene and a summary of the
speech are given, and Pen concludes:

> We glance at Mrs. Hemans' biography, and
> state where she was born, and under what
> circumstances she must have at first, etc., etc.
> Is this a correct account of Sir Barnes New-

come's lecture? I was not present, and did not read the report. Very likely the above may be a reminiscence of that mock lecture which Warrington delivered in anticipation of the Baronet's oration [66; 9:244].

That last stroke makes explicit the dubious status of evidence given this way. Pen's thoughts lead him to a remembered speech, which he gives, and then realizes that he cannot know what Barnes said, not having been there, whereupon he realizes that this scrap of memory belongs somewhere else in the chronology. The passage gives the feeling that these pieces of information are not being given in this order as steps in either a directed argument or a dramatic action, but rather as hasty attempts to explain the previous item. For instance: the confrontation between Ethel and the Colonel, which is obviously the "reason" why the scene at Mason's cottage is included, is offered as clarification for the trivial remarks of Mrs. Mason and the Colonel to each other. This is hard to explain, but easy to experience in the reading, and it is worth some efforts to clarify. We are told that Warrington has gone to Newcome to heckle Barnes at the Athenaeum, and that Clive and the Colonel have also gone to Newcome, but we do not know why. Pen tells us that "at first it was given out at Newcome that the Colonel visited the place for the purpose of seeing" Mrs. Mason [p. 241]. Our interest is entirely in why they really did come, but Pen follows the wrong thread: "Seeing Mrs. Mason" leads inevitably to a description of them seeing Mrs.

Mason. Mrs. Mason's senility is illustrated by her remarks to an anonymous lady, whose presence then must be accounted for, whereupon her behavior must be accounted for, and thus we find ourselves pulled, against our will, into a scene that insists that it be explained, and which turns out not only to be of central importance to us (if we love Ethel and the Colonel as we should), but also leads us unexpectedly to precisely where we wanted to go — Barnes' speech. Thackeray heightens the joke by promising us at the outset that he will take us there, though by his own devious ways — the chapter is entitled "In Which the Colonel and the Newcome Athenaeum are Both Lectured." John A. Lester has written about what he terms "redoublings" in Thackeray's narration (what in the movies are called "flashbacks") and he counts the redoublings in Thackeray's various novels,[5] but this passage makes it clear that the method of chronological upset is too fundamental a one in Thackeray's practice to be counted, so fundamental in fact that it is more instructive to consider his methods as based on something other than dramatic chronology than to treat it as chronology with innumerable exceptions. Clive's and the Colonel's visit to Newcome is not really to see Mrs. Mason; this fact calls to mind a remark on Mrs. Mason's state of health, which calls to mind a conversation illustrative of it, which necessitates an explanation of Ethel's presence, and so on, until Dr. Harris leads

---

[5] "Thackeray's Narrative Technique," *PMLA* (June 1954):392-409; reprinted in *Victorian Literature*, ed. Robert Preyer (New York: Harper & Row, 1966).

us to his club where the speech is being discussed, the idea of which suggests the "reminiscence" of a speech that may or may not be the right one, but which will serve.

There are other reasons why Thackeray's novels leave us with no memory of a coherent dramatic sequence. For instance, the mechanics of characters' movement and composition of place are performed by Pen either so ostentatiously or so unnoticeably, that we rightly sense that place and movement have no significance. Consider this simple example: the first half of the chapter containing Barnes' speech is taken up with a discussion among the Colonel, Clive, Pen, and some others about Barnes and what sort of treatment he deserves. It begins at the Colonel's breakfast table, with Clive and the Colonel arguing. The scene shifts: "At that moment the menaced battle is postponed. And yet I know that it must come, says poor Clive, telling me the story as he hangs on my arm, and we pace through the park" [p. 236]. The discussion continues between Clive and Pen until they arrive at Pen's house, where we learn, "It so happened that the Colonel and Mrs. Clive also called upon us that day" [p. 238], and the discussion continues without interruption until Pen introduces Warrington as an example of a differing opinion, follows him to Newcome, and so forth. If we value a strong sense of real location and movement in fiction, we might have some questions about such plot mechanics. Why do Clive and Pen go to Pen's house? Was Pen at breakfast, or had he been invited for the morning, or did he drop in? Did Clive and the

Colonel really separate for the day, both planning
to go to Pen's and with no knowledge of the other's
plans? What are the Colonel and Rosie doing today,
or any other day? Clearly these questions have no
answer. Pen, by saying that "it so happened,"
suggests the overt fortuitousness being employed
here. The change of scene in the subordinate clause
is a syntactical indication of the insignificance of
that information; that Clive is now in the park and
has left the breakfast table is as worthless a piece
of information as is the knowledge that he has
arrived at Pen's house a moment later — the Colonel arrives in the next sentence, the discussion continues, and we need never have left the morning
meal. Pen habitually indicates changes of locale
in syntactic subordination, dark corners of sentences that never get read, and consequently we
are usually without any strong sense of where our
characters are or even who precisely is present. But
even when the movement is clearly stated, we
recognize that it "just happened." When Clive and
Ethel need to see each other and neither will seek
the other out, Thackeray tells us, "It chanced that
they met in Paris, whither [Clive] went in the
Easter of the ensuing year" [45; 8:348]. When Ethel
is too confined by the attentions of her duenna,
Lady Kew, Kew decides to take the waters at
Vichy, where she stays until Thackeray wants her;
we do not remember the excuse for her absence,
because Thackeray signifies that these mechanics
of novel-writing are unrelated to the novel's meaning; never one to conceal the strokes of the artist's
brush, he calls her back with an audacious lack

of grace: "Lady Kew had got her health again, by means of the prescriptions of *some* doctors, *or* by the efficacy of *some* baths: and was again on foot and in the world" [51; 9:5, my emphasis]. This is a world where the motivation behind a character's movement is rarely more significant than a dinner invitation.

It is easy to make too much of this. If we become conscious of how much movement there is in *The Newcomes* to how little effect, how completely Thackeray's characters are without anything to do, how indistinguishable one dinner party is from another, we may be tempted to find a "theme" in it, and conclude that Thackeray is portraying dramatically the state of a society without values, and hence without valuable activities, empty of everything but nervous movement hiding the truth that all places are the same; and, while these ideas are part of his meaning, it is not with these methods that he develops it. The distinction may initially seem casuistical, but it is not: we may not conclude from the absence of information in the novel that the author intends a statement about that absence. For instance, if an author makes no mention of the physical environment of his characters, we may not posit a vision of a featureless world. Again, if Thackeray's characters never smell anything, as we will see shortly they do not, we are not justified in concluding that Thackeray means that people have no noses. Thus, when Pen shows up at Clive's breakfast table with no explanation of his coming, and when Clive and the Colonel run into each other at Pen's with no explanation of their movements,

we cannot conclude that Thackeray seeks to portray meaningless milling around, but only that such
information is not worth giving. We only sense the
meaningless milling around when we become overly
conscious of what Thackeray is not doing, whereas
Thackeray is working to keep such matters from
our attention; or, when he does bring our attention
to them, it is not as a feature of his fictional world,
but as a joke about authorship. The Colonel's
movements are without motivation, not because
his life is vacuous, but because the author can not
be bothered to manufacture any.[6]

However, if we grant that these things are not
thematically determined, we can draw more valuable conclusions. If Clive's motives for going to
Pen's house are not so much nonexistent as simply
not worth knowing, then Thackeray's meaning, in
the most general sense, is manifested in a fundamentally different way than in the classical dramatic novel, as represented best by Jane Austen, where
meaning is centered in actions and the motivations
behind them. If we do not understand perfectly
the motivation of Mr. Elton's proposal to Emma,

[6] This raises an issue with which we will always be concerned in
a discussion such as this one: the matter of rhetorical thrust. Briefly,
the question is, is Thackeray writing about his fictional world or the
processes of fiction? In this case, is the Colonel's lack of motivation
a fact about the Colonel's world or about the writing of novels? I
have been maintaining that the priorities of the latter are stronger,
and the priorities of the former are weaker, than has been realized.
As we have seen and will see again, Thackeray is willing to destroy
that world to make a point about how that world is made. Of course,
when he is at his best, as in *Vanity Fair*, the two priorities coincide;
the destruction of conventional form reinforces a moral argument.
Cf. footnotes 13 and 16, chap. 3, for a continuation of this discussion.

or Emma's visit to Miss Bates, we do not understand the novel. Precisely the meaning that Jane Austen imposes on experience is that actions such as these have moral character, in terms of their causes and consequences. That kind of meaning is rejected by Thackeray when he refuses to provide motivation for action more meaningful than a dinner invitation or a convenient attack of gout. Thackeray's meaning (as yet undefined) can be made independent of place and time, it would seem.

This is true in more extreme ways. Many of Thackeray's scenes hover between the particular and the general, further obfuscating any attempts we make to remember them in relationship to a dramatic sequence. Here is Thackeray talking about Mrs. MacKenzie's behavior in public and in private: she would batter her daughter Rosie at her piano lessons, lace her in too tightly, and descend the stair smiling, ready to beam at Rosie's public performances.

> Mamma used to cry at these ditties. "That child's voice brings tears into my eyes, Mr. Newcome," she would say. "She has never known a moment's sorrow yet! Heaven grant, Heaven grant, she may be happy! But what shall I be when I lose her!"
>
> "Why, my dear, when ye lose Rosie, ye'll console yourself with Josey," says droll Mr. Binnie from the sofa, who perhaps saw the maneuver of the widow.
>
> The widow laughs heartily and really. She places a handkerchief over her mouth. She

glances at her brother with a pair of eyes full
of knowing mischief. "Ah, dear James," she
says, "you don't know what it is to have a
mother's feelings."

"I can partly understand them," says James.
"Rosie, sing me that pretty little French song."
Mrs. MacKenzie's attention to Clive was really
quite effective. If any of his friends came to
the house, she took them aside and praised
Clive to them [23; 7:363-364].

A speech by Mrs. Mac to Mr. Honeyman is given
as an example, and Pen concludes, "And in the
interchange of such delightful remarks, and with
music and song the evening passes away." But
which evening? The shift from "used to" to the
present tense to the general "if" and back to the
present makes explicit what is less obvious in other
places — that the voices of Thackeray's characters,
as vital and striking as they are, are fixed to no
dramatic situation more specific than some evening
— or, even better, any evening, every evening. Just
as Clive's and the Colonel's debate about Barnes
goes on through breakfast and the park and Pen's
house, with the change of locale being entirely
gratuitous, so here the voice of Mrs. Mac comes
to us from a void, presented as typical behavior
any time during her pursuit of Clive for Rosie. Here
is another example, from Becky's descent into
bohemianism in *Vanity Fair*:

The behavior of the men had undergone too
I don't know what change. Grinstone showed

his teeth and laughed in her face with a familiarity that was not pleasing. . . . Tom Raikes
tried to walk into her sitting-room at the inn
with a cigar in his mouth. . . . She began to
feel that she was very lonely indeed. "If *he'd*
been here," she said, "those cowards would
never have dared to insult me." She thought
about "him" with great sadness, and perhaps
longing. . . . Very likely she cried, for she was
particularly lively, and had put on a little extra
rouge when she went down to dinner [64;
3:290].

It is a persistent feature of Thackeray's style,
that he loves to claim for his fiction exactly those
features it does not have. Thus he likes to promise
us in prefaces that his books will be full of the
swashbuckling adventure they so emphatically lack
[*VF*, "Before the Curtain;" 1:18]. So, too, in this
case. He delights in claiming a precision of temporal
and spatial immediacy, a palpable context of time
and space, which only serves to remind us that we
have had no sense of these dimensions until he
asserted their manifestness. For instance, when Pen
and Laura are returning from Brussels by boat,
there is a mention of a deck and smooth water,
and three pages of uninterrupted talk, which concludes,

"Well, we are not afraid of *you*. We are not
afraid of papa, are we darling?" This young
woman now calls out to the other member of
her family; who, if you will calculate, has just

had time to be walked twice up and down the
deck of the steamer, whilst Laura has been
making her speech about eagles [*Newc.* 66;
9:94].

The calculation, of course, cannot be made, but
we are reminded how willing we are to forget these
matters. Often Thackeray gives us a perfunctory
"Well, this is the forest of Arden," but we do not
retain it, and Thackeray is never above teasing to
remind us of the arbitrariness of the fiction: "he
walks away to his neighboring hermitage — where
have we placed it? — in Walpole Street" [11; 7:190].
And when Ethel tells Clive, "When grandmamma
comes back I shall scarcely be able to come and
see you" [50; 8:430], we are piqued that we now
must flip back through twenty-five pages to find,
in the middle of a paragraph on Lord Highgate's
new rank, a momentary parenthesis to the effect
that "When old Lady Kew was obliged to go to
Vichy for her lumbago," Highgate asked Barnes
to invite Ethel to London, whereby Ethel and Clive
could have come together [48; 8:406].

Ethel's words are false, since they imply another
kind of fictive illusion than Thackeray's — first,
they imply that imaginatively Lady Kew is any
place at all when she is not where we can see and
hear her, and secondly they imply that when she
returns Ethel will be constrained by the circumstance of her presence. But, since the movement
of characters has no moral dimension, Thackeray
can manipulate them like puppets, and the return
of Lady Kew carries no causal consequences with

it at all. Those events that potentially have consequences in the scheme of the main plot — the love
interest, for instance — are made ostentatiously
artificial by Thackeray. He makes us see that those
elements that make up a plot in *The Newcomes*
are the creation of an author who desires to make
a plot. The death of Lady Glenlivat is a famous
example. Ethel is about to make the mistake of
marrying the boorish fop Lord Farintosh, when his
mother Lady Glenlivat dies, postponing the union
until Ethel realizes her error [56]. As soon as her
death has served its purpose, she returns to life
[59; 9:141ff.]. Thackeray points out the error in his
conclusion [80; 9:429], and moments later draws
the appropriate moral regarding another instance
of such plot mechanics: "Anything you like happens in Fable-land. Wicked people die apropos (for
instance, that death of Lady Kew was most artful,
for if she had not died, don't you see that Ethel
would have married Lord Farintosh the next
week)" [p. 431]. When Thackeray has doubts about
the validity of the authorial chores he is doing, he
makes his machinery creak. Dramatic tension —
will Ethel marry a series of unattractive suitors,
or no? — is overtly manufactured.

Another manifestation of Thackeray's impulse
to acquaint us with the presence of the creator's
hand is the following: Pen is talking with Laura
about the poverty of the Newcomes and Ethel's
apparent indifference. He adds, "And now it was
that my wife told me, what I need no longer keep
secret," that Ethel, unbeknownst to all, has been
supporting Clive and the Colonel financially all this

time [76; 9:373]. In the moment of relieving the
dramatic tension, Pen reminds us that the tension
was an artificial creation by a narrator who knows
the entire story from the beginning, but who de-
ploys his knowledge to make a novel. Thackeray
can be quite blunt about this:

> I disdain, for the most part, the tricks and
> surprises of the novelist's art. Knowing, from
> the very beginning of our story, what was the
> issue of the Bundlecund Banking concern, I
> have scarce had patience to keep my counsel
> about it; and whenever I have had occasion
> to mention the company, have scarcely been
> able to refrain from breaking out into fierce
> diatribes against that ... outrageous swindle[7]
> [70; 9:297].

Thackeray is weaning us from improper literary
taste, and he is successful enough, he hopes, that
by the end of *The Newcomes* our interests have
been redirected, away from the Will-She-or-Won't-
She of conventional romance, and we can endure
his refusal to give us any ending to the drama at

[7] Wayne Booth, in *The Rhetoric of Fiction*, casts light on this
self-destruction: "One trouble with the old-fashioned methods of *Bleak
House* and *The Brothers Karamazov* is that often no reason for the
mystery is provided other than the narrator's desire to mystify. ...
Though a skillful author ... can conceal his suppressions and unveilings
pretty well, we are likely to feel cheated when we discover that facts
were held back for no good reason. ... What right has the narrator
to tell us this much and not tell us the remainder of what he knows. . . ?"
(Chicago: Univ. of Chicago Press, 1961, p. 284.) What "a skillful author"
strives to conceal, Thackeray strives to reveal — that we might become
aware of the successful concealment in others. Booth and Thackeray
are awakening the reader to the same critical insight about authorial
technique.

all. Whether Clive and Ethel marry or not, we see, is entirely the choice of an irresponsible plot-maker; Thackeray refuses to finish the busy work.

If Thackeray creates no compelling illusion of particular location, or time, or chronological sequence — if, in short, the validity of his meaning is not jeopardized by dead people not staying dead — can he be described as a realist?

Thackeray as Realist — No

All contemporary critics of Thackeray agree that his power lies in the representation of "things as they are."[8] He is described as "a daguerreotypist of the world about us" [p. 269]. His fidelity to literal fact is considered to be so complete that it jeopardizes the status of his work as art. Whitwell Elwin says in reviewing *The Newcomes*, "It is undoubtedly one of the masterpieces of English fiction, if fiction is the proper term to apply to the most minute and faithful transcript of actual life which is anywhere to be found" [p. 231]. And an anonymous critic in the *Times* says more hostilely, "He is always restricted to the domain of pure facts. He has no dreams, no superstitions, no tentative aspirations to the unseen" [p. 227]. As we have seen, Thackeray's ideas about literature share this dichotomy between the literature of the ideal, which is to him at best charming fantasy and at worst sham, and the literature of things as they are. However, this testimony to Thackeray's obedience

[8] Cf. *Thackeray, The Critical Heritage*. The page references in this paragraph are to this volume.

to literal fact is only a tribute to the success of
his illusion — for the concept of realism in art can
only be one of the creation of an illusion of the
real. Since art is by definition the alternative to
reality, an art that reproduces an artless reality
is a contradiction in terms. Realist art, then, is that
art which seeks to hide its artfulness behind the
illusion of literal reality, and this can be done in
a number of ways. We will not try to define realism,
but only apply some familiar conceptions of it to
Thackeray's art, in an attempt to isolate the source
of the realist illusion the critics found so persuasive.

We have already noticed in a number of ways
that, if, as Gandish tells us [*Newc.* 17; 7:279], "Hars
est celare Hartem," Pen as narrator seems determined to expose what art works to conceal. The
commentary on the art of the novel with which
the narrator interrupts his own performance is
familiar to all readers of *Vanity Fair* — on Amelia's
leaving Miss Pinkerton's, for instance:

> All which details, I have no doubt, JONES, who
> reads this book at his Club, will pronounce to
> be excessively foolish, trivial, twaddling, and
> ultra-sentimental. Yes; I can see Jones at this
> moment (rather flushed with his joint of mut-
> ton and half-pint of wine), taking out his pencil
> and scoring under the words "foolish, twad-
> dling," etc., and adding to them his own remark
> of "*quite true.*" Well, he is a lofty man of
> genius, and admires the great and heroic in
> life and novels; and so had better take warning
> and go elsewhere [1; 1:8-9].

The reader for a moment becomes more real than the fiction. However, though we can rightly say that Thackeray's illusion of things as they are is only one half of a paradoxical contradiction of styles, the other half being this continual declaration of the illusion's fictiveness, yet we can question the nature of the illusion itself as being, if not "unreal," at least of a rather unusual sort of realism.

First, if realism is the illusion of an unselective representation of reality, Thackeray's art is not realistic, because he is explicit about areas of experience that it does not represent, and about the artistic intentions that necessitate their exclusion [cf. chap. 1, p. 26]: intense grief, intense piety, sexual misconduct [*Newc.* 20; 7: 318] — any extremes of unambiguous vice or virtue — are eschewed as impediments to the satiric purpose.

If realism is a closeness to the soil, a concentration on the fundamental sensual aspects of life, then again Thackeray fails to qualify. With Thackeray the smell of the world is never in our nostrils; though we spend much time at the dinner table, no one ever seems to eat anything. "They marched into the apartment where the banquet was served; and which, as I have promised the reader he shall enjoy it, he shall have the liberty of ordering himself so as to suit his fancy" [*VF* 49: 2:42]. Here Thackeray makes us notice what we are missing, but usually we are untroubled by not having that area of information, because we recognize its irrelevance to his moral purposes. His treatment of charity makes this clear. Almost all of Thackeray's good women do charitable deeds, but they never seem actually to touch the poor. He tells us that charitable deeds are done, as a fact to be used in the evaluation of the doer's character, but beyond that it has no significance. Charity is done *by* people, but never *to* people. For instance, when Clara is meditating flight from her husband Barnes, who mistreats her, Laura is made ill by the thought of the impending crime, and, to explain that her reaction is not squeamishness, Pen tells us, "I have known her to tend the poor round about us, or to bear pain ... with a surprising outward constancy and calm" [57; 9:110]. But we live with Laura dramatically for three long novels, and her dramatic existence has no room for these trips to visit the poor. We may admit the fact intellectually, but it cannot exist for us dramatically. There is nothing like the oppressive effect that Tom All Alone's exercises on the world of *Bleak House*. There, that other world is a correlative, by which respectable society must eventually be measured, and incriminated. For Thackeray, it is a characterizing device: "Laura is not squeamish — here is proof."

Pickwick goes to prison and recognizes that what he sees there is an incrimination of his earlier view of the world, which could not contain it. Similarly, Laura's world view cannot contain a vision of physical fundamentals, and therefore we recognize intuitively that she has never really seen the misery of the poor. Thackeray's delicate moral distinctions must remain free of extremes of sensation which will overwhelm them, and nowhere do we see him avoiding them more clearly than when Henry Esmond goes to prison [*Esmond*, bk. 2 chap. 1]. Esmond, ward of Lord Castlewood and secretly beloved by Lady Castlewood, serves as second in a duel between Lord Castlewood and the wicked Lord Mohun over Lady Castlewood's honor. Lord Castlewood is killed, Esmond arrested and sentenced to a year in prison. Lady Castlewood, tormented with guilt at the death of a husband she did not love, blames Esmond for his death and deserts him on the eve of his imprisonment. The year in prison — an event so central to the first half of the book that it marks the division of Books One and Two, and about which Esmond says, "[My] life was changed by that stroke of the sword" which brought him there — is dispatched in three paragraphs, the heart of which is quoted here:

It was these thoughts [of Lady Castlewood's disloyalty] ... which affected Henry Esmond whilst in prison after his trial: but it may be imagined that he could take no comrade of misfortune into the confidence of his feelings. ... As a companion he was so moody and silent that the two officers, his fellow-sufferers, left him to himself mostly, ... consoled themselves with dice, cards, and the bottle, and whiled away their own captivity in their own way. It seemed to Esmond as if he lived years in that prison; and was changed and aged when he came out of it. At certain periods of life we live years of emotion in a few weeks — and look back on those times, as on great gaps

between the old life and the new. You do not
know how much you suffer in those critical
maladies of the heart, until the disease is over
and you look back on it afterwards. . . . O dark
months of grief and rage! Of wrong and cruel
endurance! He is old now who recalls you.
Long ago he has forgiven and blest the soft
hand that wounded him. . . . Esmond thought
of his early time as a novitiate, and of this
past trial as an initiation before entering into
life [10:224-225].

Prison is only a place to think — about love, loyalty,
and such matters. Where we expect a confrontation
with the physical facts of existence, we get generalized philosophy ("At certain periods of life we live
years of emotion in a few weeks"). There is not
a complete void, as when the banquet is left to
our imagination; we get a tangible piece of text
to represent the year in prison, but yet the fact
of prison never is represented. At the end of the
paragraphs on the prison term, Thackeray tells us
why those facts never materialized: "Except fresh
air, the prisoners had, upon payment, most things
they could desire. Interest was made that they
should not mix with the vulgar convicts, whose
ribald choruses and loud laughter and curses could
be heard from their own part of the prison, where
they and the miserable debtors were confined pell-
mell" [p. 226]. Thus he tells us that that realm
of experience has no place in this world, just as
he tells us when Philip loses his fortune that his
poverty will never become extreme to the point

of actual want [cf. chap. 5]. The rare exception to this rule is powerful in proportion to the implicit impossibility of its occurrence. When Amelia's household is feeling the economic pinch, she considers working, and runs smack into the real world: "Amelia thinks, and thinks, and racks her brain, to find some means of increasing the small pittance upon which the household is starving. Can she give lessons in anything? Print card-racks? Do fine work? She finds that women are working hard, and better than she can, for twopence a-day" [*VF* 50; 3:46]. That is untypical of Thackeray because it allows a moment's reflection upon those anonymous others whose sufferings are so much greater than anything his characters know, and such a reflection threatens to make his entire world appear insignificant. This may sound like a judgment against Thackeray, but it is a mistake to think it one; we need not sentence all fictional characters to Berowne's twelve months amongst "groaning wretches" and sickbeds. Some aspects of experience call forth such an overwhelmingly strong response from the reader that subtler judgments become impossible; Thackeray keeps the stench of the prison out of our nostrils, so that we may attend to more refined aspects of experience. After all, it is probably true that no moral vice elicits such a strong negative response as simple halitosis, yet few would suggest that the latter is the social critic's more worthy target.

Let us consider another way in which Thackeray's illusion of reality is not that of a classical realism. Thackeray's contemporary critics unani-

mously located his realism in the voices of his
characters — that they speak exactly like real
Englishmen. We have already noted that often
those voices speak from no particular time or place.
But we can say more. Here is an example of
Thackeray's complete realism of voice: Mr. Honeyman's chapel is becoming very popular, in spite of
the fact that it is financed by the Jewish wine
merchant, Mr. Sherrick, whose vaults are in the
basement. Thackeray records a conversation on the
subject:

> "Confound it! There are wine-vaults under the
> chapel," answers downright Charles. "I saw the
> name Sherrick and Co.; offices, a green door,
> and a brass-plate. It's better to sit over vaults
> with wine in them than coffins. I wonder
> whether it's the Sherrick with whom Kew and
> Jack Belsize had that ugly row?"
>
> "What ugly row? — don't say ugly row. It
> is not a nice word to hear the children use.
> Go on, my darlings. What was the dispute of
> Lord Kew and Mr. Belsize and this Mr. Sher-
> rick?" [11; 7:189]

If we agree that herein lies the realness of Thackeray's speakers, we must admit that it is an illusion
of reality oddly separate from any sense of individual personality; because this is a conversation
between two ciphers, a Coodle and Doodle. Just
as Mrs. MacKenzie's scene takes place on no particular evening, or on all evenings, it is not clear
which, so this conversation takes place, not be-

tween two particular people, but between every couple. The conversation happens like this:

> Members of Parliament, even Cabinet Ministers, sit under [Honeyman]. . . . The men come away from his sermons and say, "It's very pleasant, but I don't know what the deuce makes all you women crowd so to hear the man. . . . He can't make less than a thousand a year out of his chapel . . . besides the rent of the wine-vaults below the chapel."
>
> "Don't, Charles!" says his wife, with a solemn look. "Don't ridicule things in that way."
>
> "Confound it! There are wine-vaults under the chapel," etc.

Thackeray concludes the conversation with a reminder that these voices are nobody at all:

> "And what is it that enters into every row, as you call it, Charles?"
>
> "A *woman*, my love," answers the gentleman, behind whom we have been in imagination walking out from Charles Honeyman's church on a Sunday in June [p. 189].

These are the voices of their class, male and female subspecies. The voices convince, not because they are what a known personality would say, but because they are what any personality would say, within the limited range Thackeray allows himself to consider. George Henry Lewes says of his characterization, "While reading Thackeray you feel that he is painting after nature; not that he is inventing figments, nor drawing from the *repertoire*

of a worthless stage";[9] but, if Thackeray is rejecting
the stage's exhausted set of characters, he seems
to be substituting a new repertoire just as fixed.
This is "nature" in the older sense of the word —
the basic sameness that lies beneath the individualization of personal idiosyncrasy. Samuel Phillips
says, in objection to Dickens' methods of characterization by monstrosity and in praise of Thackeray's ways, "You trace something genuine in Mr.
Thackeray's figures more easily than you do in Mr.
Dickens's. You have not such a series of peculiari-
ties to separate before you can regard the nature
by itself. Fokers, Pendennises, Helens, and Lauras
abound everywhere. You can't go out without
meeting them" [*Thackeray, The Critical Heritage*,
p. 133]. Nature, then, is that which makes all men
kin; people say of Dickens's characters they wish
they could have met them; Phillips rightly says
of Thackeray's people that you meet scores of them
daily. Thackeray's schoolboys, for instance, differ
in externals, but share the same "nature." Philip
is a journalist, Clive a painter, and George Osborne
a capitalist, but they speak about their various
fields with the universal voice of Thackeray's Victorian schoolboy. Here is Clive on art: "My!
wouldn't I like to paint a picture like Lord Heath-
field in the National Gallery! *Wouldn't* I just! . . .
Wasn't Reynolds a clipper! That's all! and wasn't
Rubens a brick?" [*Newc.* 12; 7:211]. We may assume that a boy in Thackeray's world intended
for the Church would say these same words about

[9] *Thackeray, The Critical Heritage*, p. 48.

John Tillotson and Hugh Latimer. The terms change; the basic boy remains the same. Clive is Basic Boy as Artist.

Let us summarize the damage we have done to Thackeray's reputation as a realist: He lacks a minute particularity of time and place; a complete individualization of character, a complete attention to these unique people as deserving a unique sympathetic commitment from us; a nonselective inclusion of all aspects of experience; a close attention to the minutiae of daily physical existence; a strong sense of mundane fact in the sense of Defoe, where ten yards of lace for ten pounds is dubious, but nine yards, six inches of Flanders lace for six pounds ten-and-six is implicitly persuasive. But, as always, when we have pursued a line of argument so far that we are tempted to make absolute judgments, we are about to do Thackeray an injustice. We must take a new artistic perspective, one that will help us determine what Thackeray gives us as well as what he denies us.

Thackeray as Realist — Yes

E. H. Gombrich, in *Art and Illusion*,[10] in a discussion of the Greek revolution in visual art, distinguishes a kind of realism of representation that is helpful in a consideration of Thackeray. The basis of the "Greek miracle" is that a picture or other work of art offered itself as a representation, from a particular perspective, of a particular event, existing uniquely in space and time [chap. 4].

[10] Princeton: Princeton Univ. Press, 1969.

Egyptian art, on the contrary, sought to represent a man, not simply the visual image of him.

> ... as soon as the Greeks looked at the Egyptian figure type from the aspect of an art which wants to "convince," it undoubtedly raised the question why it looks unconvincing. It is the reaction we express when we speak of its "rigid posture." It might be argued that this reaction itself is due to our Greek education; it was the Greeks who taught us to ask "*How* does he stand?" or even "Why does he stand like that?" Applied to a pre-Greek work of art, it may be senseless to ask this question. The Egyptian statue does not represent a man standing rigidly or a man standing at ease — it is concerned with the what, not with the how. To ask for more might have struck an Egyptian artist as it would strike us if someone inquired the age or mood of the King on the chessboard [p. 134].

This kind of realism involves the sacrifice of what Gombrich calls "the timeless function of the potent image" [p. 138]. The Greeks make a discovery that is so familiar to us that we have difficulty seeing how odd it is: that a particular posture, a momentary mood, may be worth art's efforts to record. But we tend to forget what an enormous loss this kind of naturalism involves. The creation of a sense of perspective is gained necessarily by the denial of all information gained from all other perspectives. Thus, to give us the illusion of seeing the figure from one side, all other sides must be hidden.

To paint a man at a particular moment and in a particular mood, we must relinquish the power of representing the whole of the man in a single image. The aesthetic is one of maximal specificity at the expense of universal significance.

Whatever objections we may have to Gombrich's historical and cultural dichotomy, the distinction between two artistic processes is a helpful one. The generalizing art is represented by the parable, which avoids specificity so that its moral message may be universally applicable. Reread the story of the Prodigal Son [Luke 15:11-32] for a lesson in the power of a lack of particularizing detail. It is bare enough to be the story of every prodigal. But the novel as a genre seeks its effect through opposite means — by intensifying its illusion of particular reality — yet by doing so it renders dubious its power to instruct. The more emphatically a novel is about a certain group of fictional characters, the more emphatically it is not about anyone we know, including ourselves. Clarissa and Lovelace, for instance, persuade us of their importance by their own powerful presences, and by the power of their dramatic situation intensely realized; they need no validation as representatives of any portion of humanity larger than themselves. But, because Clarissa asks to be representative of no one other than herself, the lesson of her experience is of doubtful status for anyone else. To take a simpler example of this moral confusion at work: *Pamela*'s subtitle announces its moral lesson to be "Virtue Rewarded," or, that Virtue wins its proper reward in this life; and moralists of Richardson's time saw that Pamela's virtue was rewarded with Mr. B's hand, and they were gratified. However, the dramatic force of *Pamela* teaches us quite another lesson. The intensity of our involvement in Pamela's plight depends on our recognizing the reverse of Richardson's theme — we must see that Virtue is almost always raped and abandoned, and that only a combination of Pamela's wit and good fortune save her. It is Pamela's status as a unique individual, and not as representative of all servant girls, that complicates Richardson's moral aims.[11] A similar argument for *Clarissa* can be put forward. If we hypothesize a moral for that work like "Girls who disobey their parents and run off with men will be undone," we immediately recognize that the tragic structure necessitates that we see the situation as teaching something else, namely, that Clarissa's fall is the work of fate, and that she is entirely blameless. Or rather, as in most tragedies, her moral excellences are her undoing, and we can argue, as we can with all tragedies, that the lesson it teaches is that one should be a bit less morally uncompromising. But our point here is precisely that dramatic powers do not ask for such generalized moral judgments as a response. Clarissa represents no one but herself, and the meaning of her experience for the reader is not in terms of anyone but the novel's characters. Dramatic actions that seek to teach often resort to logically indefensible appeals to

[11] This truth is not altered if we "correct" Richardson's subtitle to "Practical Opportunism Rewarded."

sympathy — if you loved Clarissa, for her sake spare the next gentlewoman you are tempted to seduce.

The more we wonder how a realistic dramatic narrative can have significance beyond itself, the more curious the matter becomes. The difficulty is of central importance to Thackeray, because he wants his fiction to make exactly the kind of universally applicable moral statement that we have seen realist dramatic narrative makes difficult. Thus the features of Thackeray's fiction that we have thus far described seem entirely on the conceptual side of Gombrich's dichotomy between conceptual and naturalist art. But Gombrich's terms ultimately provide us with a better description of Thackeray's realism than of his abstractionism. As we noted before, the illusion of perspective is gained by the loss of all information not obtainable from that perspective. Gombrich tells us that primitive peoples have been found to be disturbed by that loss: they would rather see all four feet and both eyes of the animal than have the pleasure of recreating the visual image — and Gombrich adds that the "sacrifices of illusionism" are also the heart of Plato's distrust of art in *The Republic* [pp. 138-139]. Literature can also make this sacrifice. An author chooses a perspective from which to observe his action — Pamela's epistles, for instance — and then struggles to work in all necessary information without violating that premise; thus Pamela must write at impossible length and in unlikely situations. Thackeray creates this illusion constantly. He reminds us that his art cannot encompass all sides of his subject — that his art is precisely *a representation* of a reality of infinitely greater complexity than he can record — and by so admitting the artificiality of his art, he wins a greater belief in the reality of his subject. By asserting that his novel is rather arbitrarily excerpted from a world that extends infinitely far beyond the bounds of the book, Thackeray accomplishes something like the effect of the naturalist painter who, by omitting the far side of his figure's face, wins from the viewer a stronger belief in both the side he sees and the side he cannot see. Both the painter and Thackeray tell us a truth, so that we will believe a lie; they tell us we cannot see the other side of the face, so that we will believe it is really there.

At its most obvious, the method works like this:

> I could go on giving you interesting particulars of a hundred members of the Newcome aristocracy, were not our attention especially directed to one respectable family [55; 9:80].

> During the period which had elapsed since the Colonel's last canvassing visit ... , many things of great importance had occurred in Thomas Newcome's family — events which were kept secret from his biographer, who was, at this period also, pretty entirely occupied with his own affairs. These, however, are not the present subject of this history, which has Newcome for its business, and the parties engaged in the family quarrel there [68; 9:275].

Since the matter of the novel is excerpted from an infinite variety of equally interesting histories, Thackeray's novels turn up far more data than they can dispose of: for instance, characters are often lost sight of and Pen admits he is too rushed to tell us where they went. In *The Newcome*'s conclusion, Thackeray apologizes for the disappearance of J. J.: "Again, why did Pendennis introduce J. J. with such a flourish, giving us, as it were, an overture, and no piece to follow it? J. J.'s history, let me confidentially state, has been revealed to me too, and may be told some of these fine summer months, or Christmas evenings, when the kind reader has leisure to hear"[12] [80; 9:430]. J. J. reappears in *Philip* and again fails to capture Thackeray's attention. Since there is a novel in every man's history, and since all histories are involved with each other, characters are thrown out of the book with a forthrightness only justified by a realization that satisfying formal closure only happens in fictions. For instance, Miss Pinkerton is thrown out of *Vanity Fair*: "But why speak of her? It is probable that we shall not hear of her again from this moment to the end of time" [*VF* 1; 1:7]; her reappearance ten chapters later only underlines the degree to which this world is not under the author's control and comprehension.[13]

---

[12] The financial advantages of Thackeray's open-ended format show clearly here; he is keeping the door open on a Christmas Book.

[13] A revealing distinction can be made between such methods and the superficially similar principles of human involvement of a novelist like George Eliot. Thackeray's assertions about the interconnectedness of human destinies and the endlessness of consequence carry little

Lady Clara Newcome's dismissal from the novel's pages forces us to accept this fact about Thackeray's world, because we have become very much concerned over her fate. Thackeray refuses to tie the ends of her history. She has run off with Jack Belsize, been divorced from her husband, and we see her in squalor and irrespectability.

No wonder that her husband ... is away all day: how can he like a home which she has made wretched? In the midst of her sorrow, and doubt, and misery, a child comes to her: how she clings to it! how her whole being, and hope, and passion center itself on this feeble infant! ... but she no more belongs to our story: with the new name she has taken, the poor lady passes out of the history of the Newcomes [58; 9:133].

---

meaning for his conception of character or action; rather, it is a rhetorical device for drawing our attention to the artificiality of the book. Indeed, as we have argued, Thackeray's treatment of character suggests that consequence is easily avoided and that events are most meaningful independent of their consequences or causes. This assertion of an involvement of destinies is a sham. When George Eliot asserts, at the end of *Middlemarch*, that "every limit is a beginning as well as an ending" ("Finale"), that statement, though it is in terms of a departure from Aristotelian dramatic form, primarily exists as a statement about human experience, experience in the real world. Such assertions by Thackeray lead us not to human character, but back to the book. A similar distinction between superficially similar methods can be made concerning Thackeray's and George Eliot's use of the polemical turn to "us mortals," the readership in general, in substantiation of dramatized character. George Eliot always uses the device to underline and support her interpretation of events, whereas Thackeray, as we shall note at length later, uses that turn to obfuscate and confuse by confronting us with the distance between our ways of judging in books and in life. To repeat, then: Miss Pinkerton's banishment and reappearance is not an assertion about human experience, but rather is a rhetorical device in a continuing discussion about novel-writing.

Thus Thackeray repeatedly implies an arbitrariness in the criteria for inclusion in his novel — from a thousand equally fascinating histories, those of everyone named Newcome will be included, everyone else's excluded.

Just as characters disappear from the stage of the novel, so characters are called into existence. When Colonel Newcome is discovered to be a pensioner in Greyfriars, he explains to Pen how he got there: "... as I was walking one day upon Brighton Cliff, I met my schoolfellow, my Lord H — who has ever been a good friend of mine — " and, we are told, through his influence the Colonel was admitted [75; 9:362]. Though we never meet them, Lord and Lady H continue to show great charity toward the Colonel for the brief remainder of his life. Here is a *homo ex machina* without a doubt. The particularly Thackerayan touch is "who has ever been a good friend of mine." Thackeray can assert that Lord H has existed invisibly while the novel has been going on because he constantly reminds us that we do not see everything — that we do not see all of the Colonel, but only what Pen knows and considers relevant to the tale. Thus our hero can have lifelong friends we never hear of until a plot development necessitates our learning of them. This is true on the very largest scale: much of the events of *Pendennis*, *The Newcomes*, and *Philip* occur at the same period in Pen's life, but only glimpses of one appear in the others. When Pen interrupts *The Newcomes* to tell us he has just been married, or Clive is mentioned in *Philip*, we realize how literally true it is that other novels are happening outside one particular novel's vision. Thackeray's famous reappearing characters function to give us a peek outside the book's bounds, a hint of the reverberations the novel cannot hope to encompass.[14] When an anonymous voice at a Newcome dinner party turns out to be Dobbin [13; 7:219-222]; or when Lady Kew, Lord Steyne's sister, is driven from the field at Baden by Madame d'Ivry, her arch enemy, when Madame brings up the disgrace to the house of Steyne brought by Becky Sharp [33; 8:133], we recognize that the sense of closure that ends *Vanity Fair* is an illusion; those events are still having their repercussions. Not all of these reappearances are of any great importance — that Mr. Smee, artist, friend of Colonel Newcome's friends, and Clive's benefactor [chap. 17 and thereafter], is the selfsame Smee who was the lover of the spinster Miss Osborne in *Vanity Fair* and whose attentions angered Mr. Osborne into his daughter's enforced spinster-hood [42], may not be of much significance — but even such a small thing is a reminder that there is more to these characters' lives than the one novel can contain. Thackeray is usually quick to remind us that the only force operating for closure is the publisher's limit of three volumes.

Another means Thackeray uses to make this point is his habitual reference to times after the

[14] The extent to which Thackeray's characters appear in more than one work can only be appreciated by a perusal of *The Thackeray Dictionary*, by I. G. Mudge and Earl Sears (New York: Dutton, 1910), or the list of characters and their places of appearance in the last volume of the Kensington edition of Thackeray's works.

chronological limits of the novel, particularly the Now of the novel's writing. When Clive enters his club, Pen gives us this: " 'I am right glad to see thee, boy!' cries a cheery voice (that will never troll a chorus more)" [25; 7:404]. Fred Bayham is now dead, then, but he lives to the end of the novel, and there is not another word about his death in the book — another piece of Pen's life for which no place is ever found. Such interruptions are so destructive of dramatic intensity that we may assume they have some other purpose. The slightest touch reminds us that what we are reading about is long over and done with. Thackeray describes Clive's art studies and adds, " 'Oh,' says Clive, if you talk to him now about those early days, 'it was a jolly time!' " [16; 7:272].

Thackeray's freedom from chronology allows him to make moral points that are probably beyond the powers of a fiction strongly fixed to the dramatic present. In the midst of a ball, we learn that "the old Dowager [Lady Kew], who regularly attended all places of amusement, and was at twenty parties and six dinners the week before she died, thought fit to be particularly gracious to Madame d'Ivry upon this evening" [34; 8:155]. Or this, which switches temporal scenes and voices in midsentence to end any expectations of poetic justice within the limits of the novel: the judge at Colonel Newcome's trial for bankruptcy speaks of the Colonel's innocence, and others' guilt:

> He wished that the law had power to deal with
> those gentlemen who had come home with

> large fortunes from India, realized but a few
> years before the bankruptcy. Those gentlemen
> had known how to take care of themselves very
> well, and as for the Manager, is not his wife
> giving elegant balls at her elegant house at
> Cheltenham at this very day?[15] [71; 9:300]

But it is those interruptions without thematic
function, like the mention of Bayham's death —
interruptions that distract rather than clarify —
that, through their very lack of other function,
make us conscious of the rather arbitrary process
of selection Pen goes through to stay within his
three-volume limit.

Mrs. MacKenzie says, "You gentlemen who write
books, Mr. Pendennis, and stop at the third volume,
know very well that the real story often begins
afterwards" [23; 7:368]; thus far we have argued
that in Thackeray's world the story goes on, not
only after the novel's conclusion, but before it and
simultaneously with it, to an infinite extent. But
we can extend the terms of the argument, and say
that this is true of his world in its moral dimensions
as well as its dimensions of time and plot structure.
Just as Pen reminds us that his story and his
characters are selected from an infinite variety of
stories and character, so he reminds us that his
evaluation of those characters is just as limited;
and, just as he boasts of the arbitrariness of his
choice — (all those named Newcome are included;
there is nothing about this story to justify his

---

[15] From "as for the Manager . . . ," the voice is Pen's, speaking in
the present tense of the novel's composition.

writing it or our reading it particularly) — so he boasts of the arbitrariness of his moral judgments. He writes a novel with the Colonel as the hero and Barnes as the villain because the Colonel is his friend and Barnes is his enemy; but it could have been the other way around. In the penultimate chapter of *Philip* comes this self-destructive turn upon the narrator:

> People there are in our history who do not seem to me to have kindly hearts at all; and yet, perhaps, if a biography could be written from their point of view, some other novelist might show how Philip and *his* biographer were a pair of selfish worldlings unworthy of credit: how uncle and aunt Twysden were most exemplary people, and so forth ... — I protest, as I look back at the past portions of this history, I begin to have qualms, and ask myself whether the folks of whom we have been prattling have had justice done to them; whether Agnes Twysden is not a suffering martyr justly offended by Philip's turbulent behavior, and whether Philip deserves any particular attention or kindness at all. ... Perhaps I do not understand the other characters round about him so well, and have over-looked a number of their merits, and caricatured and exaggerated their little defects.[16] [41; 16:443-444]

[16] Again we should note that such an assertion has little meaning in terms of character for Thackeray, but much meaning in terms of the authorial role. The consequences of such a passage for a discussion of Thackeray's moral view of human nature are pernicious confusion and misunderstanding. Again, it is not an assertion about people, but about books.

And the following passage, which is ultimately more troublesome because it is openly ironic and therefore may not be avoided by calling it ironic. Pen is talking about Philip's love affair with Agnes Twysden, his older cousin, and rather inconsequently discusses the validity of the data by which we judge people:

> Don't young men always begin by falling in love with ladies older than themselves? Agnes certainly was Philip's senior, as her sister constantly took care to inform him.
>
> And Agnes might have told stories about Blanche, if she chose — as you may tell about me, and I about you. Not quite true stories, but stories with enough alloy of lies to make them serviceable coin; stories such as we hear daily in the world; stories such as we read in the most learned and conscientious history-books, which are told by the most respectable persons, and perfectly authentic until contradicted. It is only *our* histories that can't be contradicted (unless, to be sure, novelists contradict themselves, as sometimes they will). What *we* say about people's virtues, failings, characters, you may be sure is all true. And I defy any man to assert that my opinion of the Twysden family is malicious, or unkind, or unfounded in any particular. [4; 15:200]

Thus we come back to Thackeray's basic source of the realist illusion: admitting the lie of the novel, and thus asserting implicitly the reality of the novel's subject. Thou shalt have heroes and villains

— because Pen lives by his pen and must make a novel;[17] but that kind of easy characterization, like the illusion of closure at the end of the three volumes, or the creation of dramatic interest, is the product of art's distortion on a formless reality which leads neither to aesthetic satisfaction nor to moral affirmation, and Thackeray will remind us constantly of that distorting process in operation.

This standing hypothesis, that there is always more to a character than we can see, provides Thackeray with one of his most powerful devices: the ability to discover new dimensions to characters who the reader has assumed are dramatically "finished." Consider two examples. In *Vanity Fair*, when the Sedleys are ruined, they are befriended by a number of people, including the Clapps, Mr. Sedley's old clerk and his wife, who take them in as boarders [17; 1:250]. We expect to hear no more of them than we hear of "Messrs. Dale, Spiggot, and Dale, of Threadneedle Street," who remember Mr. Sedley's kindnesses and buy his silverware when it is up for auction and present it to him [1:250] — that is to say, nothing. We are mainly right. They reappear twenty-one chapters later briefly to illustrate one of Thackeray's favorite maxims. The Sedleys have settled into their new life style, and Thackeray looks in on them:

> I don't think they were unhappy. Perhaps they were a little prouder in their downfall than

[17] Cf. *Catherine* 13; 29:220; also *Virg.* 18; 12:231ff. and the discussion beginning chap. 4. Also cf. *Phil.* 35; 16:317-318.

in their prosperity. Mrs. Sedley was always a great person for her landlady, Mrs. Clapp, when she descended and passed many hours with her in the basement or ornamented kitchen. . . . She [i.e. Mrs. Sedley] stepped aside when Mrs. Rougemont the actress passed with her dubious family. She flung up her head when Mrs. Pestler, the apothecary's lady, drove by in her husband's professional one-horse chaise. . . . She counted the potatoes under the joint on Sundays, on which days, drest in her best, she went to church twice and read Blair's Sermons in the evening. [38; 2:244-245]

Aside from a few such references, the Clapps remain invisible while the Sedleys suffer through their domestic difficulties, and the reader is secure in his perception of the Clapps' limited dramatic function. When Amelia is being rescued from poverty and is moving out of the Clapps' cottage, the Clapps again serve as mere yes-men, an easy mechanical substantiation of the narrator's characterization of others: "They could not recall a harsh word that had been uttered by Amelia. She had been all sweetness and kindness. . . . They never would have such lodgers again, that was quite clear" [59; 3:212]. But on the next page we discover that there were novels'-worths of high emotion going on within those walls that we never saw.

Poor Emmy's days of happiness had been few in that humble cot. . . . She never liked to go back to the house after she had left it, or to face the landlady who had tyrannized over her when ill-humored and unpaid, or when pleased had treated her with a coarse familiarity scarcely less odious. ... In the vulgar sycophant who now paid court to her, Emmy always remembered the coarse tyrant who had made her miserable many a time, when the rent was overdue; who ... had seen her humble and trampled upon her.

Nobody ever heard of these griefs, which had been part of our poor little woman's lot in life. She kept them secret. [213-214]

How we deal with this depends on how much we are willing to claim for Thackeray's artistry. If we assume that he is successful with this, that it is more than his being self-contradictory, we can only make sense of the first passage in light of the second by honoring the author's professions of partial vision, open prejudice, and the like. We need not maintain that Thackeray conceives of Mrs. Clapp's meanness and keeps it hidden from us so that he may make the thematic assertion that there is more to Mrs. Clapp than her dramatic function as benefactor to the Sedleys can contain. We need only say that Thackeray creates the potential for such revaluations, and even for such self-contradictions, by his repeated reminders that he only knows so much, that he has not the time or space to tell all of what he knows, that his information is biased both as he receives it and as he retells it, and finally that matters of accuracy and authenticity are sacrificed to the primary concern, that of making a marketable novel. That Mrs. Clapp is being used by Thackeray to a very limited dramatic purpose (until she bursts through those limitations in the second passage) does not prohibit for him the existence of a full personality and a full life for her.

Of course, this is all a sham; but it is a testament to the excellence of Thackeray's sham that, by discussing openly the processes of his art at work upon his world, we are led to discuss his novels in terms of a dichotomy between his art and the real world it distorts. Thus we have discussed Mrs. Clapp in terms of his dramatic use of her, and the real person who is a little too big to fit into such a small role. And there lies a critical pitfall at the end of all this. We have two novels, which correspond to what Pen would call real life and the novel he is writing from it, or the novel that Thackeray is writing and the one Pen is writing. Often this distinction is absolutely clear, as at the end of *Catherine*, where Ikey Solomons' text ends, a line is drawn, and Thackeray's voice discusses for a few pages "what Solomons has done"; or at the end of *The Newcomes*, when Pen's portion ends, a line is drawn, and Thackeray tells us how the story happened to come to him. But the dichotomy is ever operative to varying degrees throughout the novels. The problem is this: Pen's novels are quite conventional and rather bad — they are novels of heroes and villains; whereas Thackeray's novels are less artful but better, and repeatedly assert themselves to disrupt the conventional patterns of Pen's novels. Thus we have a narrator who makes less of his novels than they are, and novels that seem to sport excellences of which the narrator is unaware. This becomes a critical problem when we seek to determine Thackeray's moral vision, because Pen often speaks in terms of a moral absolutism and simplicity that the experience of the novel belies.

The development of Mrs. MacKenzie is a good example of how the dramatic role in the scheme of Pen's novel proves inadequate to contain the full character. When she is pursuing Clive for her daughter Rosie, everyone whose opinion is valuable agrees that she is "a merry woman," and so obviously disingenuous that she is delightful [23]. She is like Mrs. O'Dowd of *Vanity Fair*, matchmaking for her rather sorry daughter with a fine, hilarious disregard for the truth. She is a comic figure, because she is so obvious that she poses no threat. But something goes awry, Clive marries Rosie at the request of his father, and Mrs. MacKenzie changes.

Had Clive become more knowing in his travels, had Love or Experience opened his eyes, that they looked so differently now upon objects which before used well enough to please them? It is a fact that, until he went abroad, he thought widow MacKenzie a dashing, lively, agreeable woman. [43; 8:409]

It was surprising what a change appeared in the Campaigner's conduct, and how little, in former days, Colonel Newcome had known her. [63; 9:204]

Warrington correctly decides that she is now "an ogling, leering, scheming, artful old campaigner" [43; 8:312]. She becomes ultimately something much worse, and murders the Colonel with her persecution. That metamorphosis should be impossible, just as it would be impossible for Peggy O'Dowd to become truly evil. On what grounds do we assume that that is so? There is some way in which her comic presentation as a merry and absurd woman should rule out that kind of development. It appears as if she is called upon to play a part Pen's characterization of her simply has not prepared her to play; just as Rowena was followed from the joust into the kitchen and found to be incomplete, so Mrs. MacKenzie cannot be the mother-in-law of an impoverished Clive within the simple limits of that character, so more of her character appears. The error that Pen, Warrington, Clive, the Colonel, and the reader make is based on an assumption about novelistic propriety: that a character's characterization will be suitable and adequate for what he or she has to do. In this case, the character of "merry woman" is perfectly adequate to Mrs. Mac's role as comic threat to Clive's union with Ethel, but she finds herself impoverished and tied to the quixotic Colonel, and she must become the Campaigner. Everyone assumes that, because Mrs. Mac is a "merry woman," she is always and only a merry woman. That is not an assumption one makes from one's knowledge of people, but from one's knowledge of books. Thackeray's violations of dramatic structure remind us that our criteria for judgment within the novel are aesthetic rather than moral.

Disobeying the Implications of Dramatic Form, and a Comparison with Dickens

The illusion that Thackeray works to create, that of a real world more extensive, interconnected, and morally ambiguous than the author can deal with, and especially more so than the conventional romantic novel can represent, is made clearer by a consideration of Dickens' opposite aesthetic. When Mr. Pickwick rises in the dawn of his novel and opens his window, he sees an emblem of Dickens' world of complete artistic control: "Goswell Street was at his feet, Goswell Street was on his right hand — as far as the eye could reach, Goswell Street extended on his left; and the opposite side of Goswell Street was over the way" [*Pickwick Papers*, chap. 2]. The creator assures us at the outset that in this world all Goes Well. The difference in the two sets of assumptions shows if we use the old technique of imagining the characters living between scenes. Thackeray typically tells us that he does not know what his people do off the stage of the novel, or that he knows and it would make a good story if he had time to tell us. Dickens' characters are frozen in an eternal present participle. In *Great Expectations*, Pip leaves Magwitch on the marshes hugging himself and limping about. He returns: "there was the right man — hugging himself and limping to and fro, as if he had never all night left off hugging and limping" [chap. 3].

Dickens is a particularly good contrast to Thackeray, because his moral meaning is so completely involved with artistic determinism and control, and thus he throws light on the problems Thackeray raises for himself when he denies himself that control. *Great Expectations*, for instance, makes a moral statement about people in society — that they are inextricably involved with each other, either as brothers in love or partners in crime, and they must choose which it is to be. Thus the discovery of a relationship of blood and deed between Magwitch and Stella is not a coincidence but a moral inevitability, and it is a measure of Pip's moral blindness that he thinks that what is most feared and what is most wanted in his world can be kept separate. Magwitch and Stella are inevitably related, then, as inevitably as Ahab is to meet his whale — but why? Dickens would have it that that inevitability is a moral truth, but really it is an artistic one — that this novel is a work of art and is constructed to some artistic purpose. In this sense, *Great Expectations* (and Dickens's other late novels) takes much of its dramatic push forward from the desire to discover the relationships between apparently unrelated people and events, relationships that will explain the presence of these people and events and no others in the same novel. The basic mystery to be revealed then is, why are all these elements brought together under one cover? When that question is answered, and the total artfulness of the structure revealed, the books end.

This most basic of assumptions — that this is
a work crafted to an artistic purpose — is one that
Thackeray denies us. Though the proprieties of the
novelistic art may be hard to define, it is easy to
sense that Thackeray is disobeying them. For instance, a character's death scene should have rhetorical weight proportional to his dramatic importance; yet Major Pendennis has been with us for
eight hundred pages of *Pendennis,* where he dom-
inates the book and we grow to love him, and
for two-thirds of *The Newcomes* when Pen, in the
midst of Clara Newcome's contemplated running
away from her brutal husband Barnes and in the
process of defining Laura's moral revulsion from
Clara, gives us one short paragraph telling us that
the Major is soon to die and that he blessed Laura
as an angel on his deathbed [49; 8:423]; that is,
one of our heroes dies and we are told about it
as illustrative of Laura's character regarding another set of events.

Another example of dramatic impropriety: Clive
returns from Rome upon hearing that Ethel's engagement has been broken off. Pen attempts to
dissuade him by describing the awful social heights
Clive is attempting to scale. Empty names doing
empty things follow in Thackeray's most glittering
style:

My dear Clive ... do you know to what you
are aspiring? For the last three months Miss
Newcome has been the greatest lioness in London. ... Miss Blackcap, Lady Blanche Blackcap's daughter was (as perhaps you are not
aware) considered by her mamma the great

beauty of last season. . . . This year Farintosh
will not look at Miss Blackcap! . . . Then, my
dear fellow, there were, as possibly you do not
know, Lady Hermengilde and Lady Iseult,
Lady Rackstraw's lovely twins, whose appearance created such a sensation at Lady Haut-
bois' first — was it her first or was it her second?
— yes, it was her second —breakfast. . . .
Crackthorpe was mad, they said, about both
— Bustington, Sir John Fobsby . . . the Bishop
of Windsor was actually said to be smitten with
one of them. . . . Where is Bustington? Where
is Crackthorpe? Where is Fobsby, the young
Baronet of the North? My dear fellow, when
those two girls come into a room now, they
make no more sensation than you or I. Miss
Newcome has carried their admirers away
from them. [41; 8:267-268]

And so it continues. "Where is Bustington?" It is
a joke, like the precise concern over first and second
breakfasts, emphasizing the very limited reality
status such an evocation of a world has. Bustington
is nowhere, because he is only a name, without the
believability that suggests a physical location. But
where is Crackthorpe? He is in chapter 43 and
following, having become a close friend of Clive's
and an active participant in the drama. It is as
if one of Dickens's Boodles and Coodles came to
life and starred in his own novel.

There are countless other examples of Thackeray's violating the principles of his own drama.[18]

---

[18] Cf. *The Yellowplush Papers*, where pure farce turns to utter horror
on the last page.

In *Philip,* Thackeray promises us times of poverty and want for hundreds of pages, times that finally arrive and last for two pages [40; 16:436-439 — "Their griefs were drawing to an end now"]. In *The Newcomes,* the sentimental reunion between Clive and his father after years apart is replaced with a parody of G. P. R. James' opening scenes [51]. In *Vanity Fair,* Thackeray calmly philosophizes on evidence that he tells us a page later is false [40; 2:279-280] (this passage is discussed fully on pp. 171-172). These things should be impossible. There should come a time in the pursuit of verisimilitude when an authorial pause for a G. P. R. James parody can no longer be tolerated; Thackeray never senses that prohibition.[19] At least when an author moralizes on the action of his novel he should not be able to tell us on the next page that that action did not really occur. All these things Thackeray does, as well as the grand violation of dramatic structure that we have been dealing with all along — his refusal to write his novel's conclusion. Thackeray may be approaching, or indeed be well over, a precipice; for, though the appearance of artlessness is necessary to a strong realistic power, just as essential to an intelligent reading is the assumption of artfulness — "it just happened" can never be an admissible explanation. Thackeray's novels cultivate a convincing appearance of such reasonless fortuitousness; if they succeed, so that "it just happened" is the best explanation of his pages, Thackeray and literary criticism had best have done with each other.

[19] The exception to this rule, and to this discussion in general, is *Esmond,* which will be dealt with as an exception in chap. 5.

Let us seek a relocation of his value. If his works can survive such things as we have seen here — and many feel they cannot — then we must admit that the terms by which these works define their value must not be the ones we, through custom, assume them to be — unity of action, for instance. These books must rest on other supports, if they can kick away these familiar ones and still stand. To find out what holds them up, we must turn from the narrative, where we have found no peace, to the narrator.

4: The Narrative Voice

It is often felt that Thackeray's obtrusive narrator is an obstacle to the enjoyment of his novels; however, by now we have seen that the conventional orientation toward narrator and narrative, which considers the teller something to be looked past, and the tale the thing to be looked at, does not work here. Thackeray's commentary on his fiction is so large a part of his work that to attempt to look past it as some sort of vehicle for telling a story is to ignore what to him is often primary. And even more — if we do succeed in looking past that voice to the novel it is telling, we will find the unsatisfying, confused congeries the previous chapter has examined. The narrator's novels are not very good; his commentary on them can be excellent. This chapter will examine the properties of that voice, eventually defining the use of the novel that the narrator by example is suggesting we make.

The Dissertation on the Novel

We have seen that Thackeray's novels often refuse to obey the implicit commands of their own

conventional form. An alternative to that outright
rebellion from convention is for Pen to give us what
convention demands, but to preface it with a discussion of novel writing, the demands of convention
and a conventional public, and similar subjects.
The method is basic to *Catherine*, where Thackeray
prefaces his bloody consummation with a long
denunciation of anyone who might like it and the
literary customs that require it [13; 29:219-220]. In
The Virginians, when Pen must write a love scene,
we get pages, not of the scene itself, but of Pen's
desire not to write it.

> Any man or woman with a pennyworth of
> brains, or the like precious amount of personal
> experience, or who has read a novel before,
> must, when Harry pulled out those faded vege-
> tables just now, have gone off into a digression
> of his own, as the writer confesses for himself
> he was diverging whilst he has been writing
> the last brace of paragraphs. . . . When, I say,
> a lad pulls a bunch of amputated and now
> decomposing greens from his breast and falls
> to kissing it, what is the use of saying much
> more? . . .
>   And how came Maria to give it to Harry?
> And how did he come to want it and to prize
> it so passionately when he got the bit of rub-
> bish? Is not one story as stale as the other?
> Are not they all alike? What is the use, I say,
> of telling them over and over? . . . The incidents
> of life, and love-making especially, I believe
> to resemble each other so much, that I am
> surprised, gentlemen and ladies, you read

> novels any more. Psha! Of course that rose in
> young Harry's pocket-book had grown, and
> had budded, and had bloomed, and was now
> rotting, like other roses. I suppose you will
> want me to say that the young fool kissed it
> next? Of course he kissed it, . . .

and so on [18; 12:231-232]. This writing about
writing, this eye upon himself as author, becomes
more pronounced in Thackeray's writings until it
reaches the following apotheosis in *Philip*: Philip
has lost his job at the Pall Mall Gazette, and Pen's
thoughts turn to the economics of journalism:

> Ah how wonderful ways and means are! When
> I think how this very line, this very word,
> which I am writing represents money, I am
> lost in a respectful astonishment. . . . I am paid,
> we will say, for the sake of illustration, at the
> rate of sixpence per line. With the words, "Ah,
> how wonderful," to the words, "per line," I can
> buy a loaf, a piece of butter, a jug of milk,
> a modicum of tea. . . . Wife, children, guests,
> servants, charwoman, we are all making a meal
> off Philip Firmin's bones as it were. [35;
> 16:317-318]

It is this apparent willingness to destroy the novel
to make a point about the business of reading and
writing that makes us realize that we cannot look
past that voice as we look past the frame of a
picture to the imagined reality beyond. Thackeray's last group of essays, *The Roundabout
Papers*, makes this clear. Written when Thackeray
was editor of the *Cornhill Magazine* in the years

immediately before his death, they are largely about the writing of essays, these essays particularly. "On Two Roundabout Papers Which I Intended to Write" is paradoxically the treatment of two subjects to show how completely unsuitable they are as essay topics; "On a Joke I Once Heard from the Late Thomas Hood" is about Thackeray's refusal to tell us the joke. "On Two Children in Black" is not so much about the children themselves as about Thackeray's right to write about them, even though there is no story to be told. It is an essay on the nature of the essay, using itself as an object for discussion — just as we have been maintaining that his novels use the conventional novel within themselves to make a point about novels and the assumptions about life that go into and come out of them. In these last essays, Thackeray begins with a defense of his right to be unorganized, egocentric, and trivial, and goes on to discuss the nature and responsibilities of the writer and reader. Here is a sample:

> *Linea recta brevissima.* That right line "I" is the very shortest, simplest, straightforwardest means of communication between us, and stands for what it is worth and no more. . . . When this bundle of egotisms is bound up together, as they may be one day, if no accident prevents this tongue from wagging, or this ink from running, they will bore you very likely; so it would to . . . eat up the whole of a ham: but a slice on occasion, may have a relish: a dip into the volume at random and so on for

> a page or two: and now and then a smile; and
> presently a gape: and the book drops out of
> your hand: and so, *bon soir*, and pleasant
> dreams to you. [27:12-13]

The authorial self-awareness which these examples
represent in its most overt form trains a similar
objective critical scrutiny in the reader. Thackeray
teaches us to attend to the rhetorical and dramatic
processes of the novel as we experience them. The
reader must share Thackeray's awareness of the
artistic process; ultimately the degree of insight
into the inner workings of fiction granted to the
reader by Thackeray, and expected from him, is
a very high one.

> Who knows any one save himself alone? Who,
> in showing his house to the closest and dearest,
> doesn't keep back the key of a closet or two?
> I think of a lovely reader laying down the page
> and looking over at her unconscious husband,
> asleep, perhaps, after dinner. Yes, madam, a
> closet he hath: and you, who pry into every-
> thing, shall never have the key of it. I think
> of some honest Othello pausing over this very
> sentence in a railroad carriage, and stealthily
> gazing at Desdemona opposite to him, inno-
> cently administering sandwiches to their little
> boy — I am trying to turn the sentence off
> with a joke, you see — I feel it is growing too
> dreadful, too serious. [*Newc.* 11; 7:192]

Thackeray's intrusions are either infuriating or
delightful, depending on whether we want to experience the fictive illusion or study it. Thackeray

wants us to recognize, first, that Othello in a railroad carriage is rather absurd, and second, that the narrator is using that absurdity to avoid a darkness of moral vision that would violate the spirit of a light comedy of manners. He teaches us to attend to the distance between the verbal surface and the real meaning, the rhetorical effect and the means of achieving it, and it is this that makes Thackeray's novels demonstrably greater than Pen's evaluation of them. Thackeray gives us the tools by which we can come to a truer evaluation of the novel than Pen does.

The Undercutting of Conventional Rhetoric

Thackeray began his career as a parodist of style [cf. the *Novels by Eminent Hands*], and he remains always supremely conscious of the distortive effect of style on subject matter; he habitually makes his meaning felt by the exaggeration of conventional rhetoric until its failure to describe accurately becomes unmistakable. When Barnes and his father discuss restraining the editorial hostility of the *Newcome Independent*, the liberal paper, Pen comments, "during the above conspiracy for bribing or crushing the independence of a great organ of British opinion, Miss Ethel Newcome held her tongue" [14; 7:246]. "Great organ of British opinion" rings false enough to cause us to pause and consider the facts, which suggest that the paper is as unprincipled and selfish as the Newcomes. When Clive and Rosie are making their ill-conceived marriage, the source of the allusion directs

our attention below the surface: "So, as a good
thing when it is done had best be done quickly,
these worthy folks went off almost straightway to
a clergyman, and were married out of hand" [62;
9:190, cf. *Macbeth* 1; 7:1]. Frequently the language
represents the spirit of the actors — "great organ
of British opinion" is the newspaper's own conception of itself — and it reflects the actor's distorted
self-image. Clive, for instance, when he is struggling
to understand his love for Ethel, describes it entirely in a language taken from romantic art — ballad,
novel, classical epic, and so on [cf. 30; 8:77, 76, and
43; 8:307] — and that use of an artificial language
is definitely an attempt to take refuge in convention. Clive claims for his love a conventional heroic
status it does not deserve. When J. J. tries to make
him face the practical problems of courting above
one's station with no money, Clive sings, "Her heart
it is another's, she never-can-be-mine"; but Ethel
is struggling with real-life problems she knows the
romances cannot help her solve. Her heart is not
another's; rather the barriers are the less romantic
ones of birth, wealth, and profession.

And as the rhetoric of the romance is undercut,
so the rhetoric of the pulpit is questioned by using
it to deliver the narrator's best cynicism. Here is
the conclusion of his description of the miseries
of the Steyne household in Vanity Fair: "So . . .
it is very likely that this lady [i.e. Steyne's wife],
in her high station, had to . . . hide many secret
griefs under a calm face. And let us, my brethren
who have not our names in the Red Book, console
ourselves by thinking comfortably how miserable

our betters may be" [47; 3:6]. The religion of righteous self-congratulation is uncovered. As with Clive's use of the rhetoric of romance, the presence of rhetoric represents an attempt to hide an unpleasant truth under an attractive surface, and Thackeray makes sure that it fails. An interesting nonverbal manifestation of this use of convention is in the illustrated majuscules which begin the chapters. They often illustrate, not the story, but the conventional images, drawn from myth and romance, in which the actors see the story. Chapter 69, in which the Colonel gains his revenge against Barnes by defeating him in the parliamentary election, by the wholly unethical means of Fred Bayham and company, is headed with the Colonel's image of the affair, which the chapter belies — two knights jousting [9:259].

However, Thackeray's use of rhetoric is not as completely under control as we have so far suggested. That he uses rhetoric and undercuts it, everyone knows who reads his novels; but that he does so to any determinable purpose, one is not so sure. This problem has probably resulted in more critical dissatisfaction with Thackeray than any other, a dissatisfaction that is usually inadequately expressed by saying that Thackeray seems to be laughing at everything. John Forster says, in a review of *Vanity Fair*, "we are seldom permitted to enjoy the appreciation of all gentle and kind things which we continually meet with in the book, without some neighboring quip or sneer that would seem to show the author ashamed of what he yet cannot help giving way to."[1] Robert Bell also suggests some inner conflict: "He cannot call up a tear without dashing it off with a sarcasm. Yet his power of creating emotion is equal to his wit, although he seems to have less confidence in it, or to have an inferior relish for the use of it."[2] This is the role of sentimental cynic, in which Thackeray has so long been cast.[3] We now have the insight necessary to put to sleep some of the myth. Thackeray's lack of conviction about the value of extreme sensibility is rather a lack of conviction about such feelings fictively aroused. No one who knew Thackeray personally suggests that he had any doubts about the value of tears, but he tells us in his fiction openly that he has severe doubts about the value of tears shed for heroines in books. He does like to dash away our tears, but usually with a reminder that our uncomplicated sympathy is a luxury provided by the pleasing distortions of romance.

But the critics are in spirit right; Thackeray undercuts his own rhetoric as well as the rhetoric of his characters, and in ways for which we cannot offer explanation or defense except in the general terms of an habitual ironic perspective. We know that he is being "ironic," without any sure knowledge of what the irony is meant to point to. We do not know what Thackeray means; we only know

---

[1] *Examiner*, 22 July 1848, 468-470; reprinted in Tillotson and Hawes, eds., *Thackeray, The Critical Heritage*, p. 54.

[2] *Fraser's*, Sept. 1848, 320-333; reprinted in *Thackeray, The Critical Heritage*, p. 65.

[3] Cf. Lambert Ennis' *Thackeray, The Sentimental Cynic* (Evanston: North-western Univ. Press, 1950).

for sure that he does not mean what he says. In
fact, we do not even know that for sure, as we shall
see. Consider this description of the Brighton
beach:

> Along the rippled sands (stay, are they rippled
> sands or shingly beach?) the prawn-boy seeks
> the delicious material of your breakfast.
> Breakfast — meal in London almost unknown,
> greedily devoured in Brighton! In yon vessels
> now nearing the shore the sleepless mariner
> has ventured forth to seize the delicate whit-
> ing, the greedy and foolish mackerel, and the
> homely sole. [*Newc.* 9; 7:146]

Once we recognize the artificiality of the rhetoric,
what explanation for it can we offer? When Thackeray slips into blank verse, can we say why? This
is foolery only, but our very point is that no
dramatic moment is free from the potential for
such.[4] We can make matters worse: If we explain
the allusion to *Macbeth* quoted above as a directive
to a moral interpretation of the marriage, how do
we explain it when we discover it used repeatedly
by Thackeray in the most innocent situations?
Pen's use of allusion, then, is often morally equivalent to Clive's — as a "pre-fab" response to a situation, one that allows the user to avoid a personal moral involvement with the particulars.
As the next paragraphs will show, convention is
a mask, and, while both Clive and Pen are quick

---

[4] Cf. pp. 161-162, for one example and further discussion, and cf.
footnote 9, chap. 2, and footnote 6, chap. 4, and the passages they
discuss for other esamples.

to acknowledge the existence and artificial nature of the mask, it still successfully allows them to avoid having to confront the face in the mirror.

Thackeray's enjoyment of artificial styles for their own sake, and without specific ironic intent, causes the critic serious problems. Here is the best of Thackeray's critics looking for a sure reading of perhaps the central passage in Thackeray's best book; failure here would have most serious implications indeed. The scene is Rawdon's confrontation with Becky and Lord Steyne; the critic is John Loofbourow.[5]

> In the discredited context of criminal romance, a farcical Satan and a melodramatic Eve have played a primordial scene for laughs. The fallen Becky — "wretched woman" ... "brilliants on her breast which Steyne had given her." ... "I am innocent." ... "All covered with serpents, and rings, and baubles." Steyne, the Tempter — "hanging over the sofa" ... "grinding his teeth" ... "fury in his looks." The "bald forehead" of the second-rate serpent is bruised by the clumsy Adam, Rawdon — "Steyne wore the scar to his dying day." In the parodic context, this biblical sequence is a moral nightmare.

Loofbourow is saying that Thackeray, by the use of a discredited rhetoric, alerts us to the distance between the verbal surface and the true moral nature of the scene. The rhetoric of criminal ro-

---

[5] *Thackeray and the Form of Fiction* (Princeton: Princeton Univ. Press, 1964) pp. 25-26.

mance and the biblical machinery is a purposely
noisy attempt to simplify the moral ambiguities
of this moment, when all the challenges *Vanity Fair*
makes to our complacency are becoming explicit.
The rhetoric attempts to cast the characters as
heroes and villains, and the artificiality of tone
alerts us to that distortion as it is done. Becky's
serpentine jewelry is an example of Thackeray's
sense of a deluding style, of the lying power of the
symbol — because Becky is not simply evil, though
the scene is more comfortable to read if she is so
cast.

Though this interpretation of Loofbourow's is
fundamentally correct, it ignores a problem it
raises. The rhetoric of this scene is certainly "discredited," or at least questioned, by Thackeray, but
we have argued that Thackeray discredits all languages; thus the reader's task is not to determine
whether or not the language at hand has been
discredited — at which point he may conclude the
passage to be "parodic" — but rather to determine
how to establish criteria for evaluation of texts that
are inevitably in one or another discredited rhetoric. Loofbourow implies that we reject the superficial reading of this scene because we recognize the
presence of a discredited rhetoric; but the rhetoric
only directs us to evaluate its assertions in the
context of the novel; the novel proves the scene
simplistic — the false rhetoric only asks us to find
criteria for judgment other than itself. The distinction may seem small when dealing with a scene
that in either system is a fraud, but when the scene
is apparently legitimate the distinction becomes

critical. Consider these passages, both in a "discredited" rhetoric, but neither revealing a "moral nightmare" behind the words.

And this, at the end of threescore and seven or eight years, was to be the close of a life which had been spent in freedom and splendour, and kindness and honor; this the reward of a noble heart — the tomb and prison of a gallant warrior who had ridden in twenty battles — whose course through life had been followed by blessing, and whose career was to end here — here — a low furious woman standing over him and stabbing the kind defenseless breast with killing insult and daily outrage! [*Newc.* 73; 9:328]

The painter turned as he spoke; and the bright northern light which fell upon the sitter's head was intercepted, and lighted up his own as he addressed us. ... The palette on his arm was a great shield painted of many colors: he carried his maul-stick and a sheaf of brushes along with it, the weapons of his glorious but harmless war. With these he achieves conquests, wherein none are wounded save the envious: with that he shelters him against how much idleness, ambition, temptation! Occupied over that consoling work, idle thoughts cannot gain the mastery over him; selfish wishes or desires are kept at bay. Art is truth: and truth is religion; and its study and practice a daily work of pious duty. [*Newc.* 65; 9:231-232]

Clearly we need a more flexible way to deal with
rhetoric than simply to divide it into two categories,
discredited and still-undiscredited. Because it is a
prominent feature of Thackeray's fiction that languages that have been "discredited" are somehow
still available for use, and to great effect, as in the
passage about Colonel Newcome quoted above. It
is more helpful to say that Thackeray teaches us
to scrutinize all styles, to look behind them and
test them against a larger moral context; what is
finally being discredited is not so much a language
or languages, but the authorial process as an evaluative instrument. Rhetoric, in the most general
sense, is being questioned: the use of persuasive
language by an enthusiastic and short-sighted author to enforce his interpretation of fictive events
upon the reader surreptitiously. Thackeray indicates surely that sometimes what his narrator says,
or how his narrator interprets, is not the truth;
it would seem that there is no logical end to that,
and that once the question of authorial insincerity
has been raised, all rhetoric must be tested with
some correlative. Thackeray, by admitting that the
rhetoric of his narrator is of dubious value, implies
that there is some basic substratum of truth that
rhetoric obscures, and that we have some means
to determine that truth. This, however, is not
obviously so. Wayne Booth, in *The Rhetoric of
Fiction*, argues persuasively against the basic realist myth that fictive experience is somehow self-
evaluative and that therefore the author should
strive to remove himself as much as possible from
the work and let it make its own meaning. As Booth

observes, the ideal dichotomy between matter and
manner is based on the fallacy that one is truer
than the other. Both are equally fictional, and thus
indistinguishable. Booth gives evidence for the confusion that arises when authors deny the reader
sure rhetorical directives. Thackeray is between
two stools — he neither gives us sure rhetorical
directives, nor denies us rhetorical directives at all;
rather he gives us the rhetoric and questions it.
This makes him rather unique in Booth's scheme,
because if an absence of rhetoric leads to confusion
and unreadability, then Thackeray is made somewhat readable by his rhetoric, even if it is a specious
sense of order that it brings.

One must learn to read back and forth between
Thackeray's "realist" moral vision and his authorial commentary. Simply to discard the latter is
to distort his work competely; to contain the two
in one reading is difficult indeed. Becky's serpentine
jewelry is a good instance of the difficulties involved. If we assume, as we did previously, that
the serpentine symbolism is a fraud, designed to
awaken us, by its convenient artificiality, to the
moral ambiguities of her situation the symbol fails
to represent, we are forced to "throw out" of *Vanity
Fair* the large amount of text in which Thackeray
describes Becky as simply evil. The famous mer-
maid metaphor at the beginning of Becky's dark
history, for instance:

In describing this syren, singing and smiling,
... the author, with modest pride, asks his
readers all round, has he once forgotten the

laws of politeness, and showed the monster's
hideous tail above water? No! Those who like
may peep down under waves that are pretty
transparent, and see it writhing and twirling,
diabolically hideous and slimy, flapping
amongst bones, or curling round corpses. [64;
3:285]

The question is, do we take the opportunity
Thackeray gives us to say that this is a joke (". . .
we had best not examine the fiendish marine canni-
bals, revelling and feasting on their wretched *pick-
led* victims," my emphasis), and thus forget it?
Thackeray will always give us that opportunity,
but there is no end to that, and if we laugh at
this we will laugh always and never know when
to stop laughing.[6] It is this lack of confidence with
which we take in his fiction that disturbed his
contemporary critics and made them suspect they
were being laughed at. This is perhaps the most
fundamental way in which his fiction is confused
and thus forgettable — because we never have
complete confidence in the manner of our involvement with the text. Because, just as we have seen
that the central moment of high drama in *Vanity
Fair* is meant to discredit itself through the very
height of the drama, similarly the presence of a
joke does not mean the passage is meant to be
funny — as we saw in the passage about Othello

[6] Cf. the passage quoted on p. 31. The "whizz" is the essence of
Thackeray's style — it flaunts his independence from his own emotion,
and offers the reader the opportunity to escape the effect of his intense
seriousness.

in the railroad carriage, where Thackeray tells us he is trying to be funny and achieves a moment of high seriousness by doing so.

Let us take George Osborne's death scene and seek an absolute authority among the various languages used to describe it. We begin with Jos showing the white feather [32; 2:145ff.]. In two paragraphs George is dead. Jos' farcical cowardice is followed by a paragraph on the atrocity of war: "There is no end to the so-called glory and shame, and to the alternations of successful and unsuccessful murder, in which two high-spirited nations might engage." Then one paragraph in a magnificent heroic style: "unscared by the thunder of the artillery, which hurled death from the English line — the dark rolling column pressed on and up the hill. . . . Then it stopped, still facing the shot. Then at last the English troops rushed from the post from which no enemy had been able to dislodge them." Then the neutral announcement that "Amelia was praying for George, who was lying on his face, dead, with a bullet through his heart." The next chapter begins with the worldly Miss Crawley reading the promotions resulting from the battle in the Gazette, and speculating on Rawdon's chances, and missed chances, for advancement. We go from comedy to bitter philosophy to heroism to social pragmatism in five paragraphs, with George's death in the middle, surrounded by these alternative evaluations of the military drama in which he has been acting that fatal role. Is Jos right to run, if the battle was only "so-called glory and shame" and "successful and unsuccessful murder"? "So-called" implies that the battle is called glory and shame falsely — what is it truly called? Can a soldier be heroic in the doing of wicked deeds? Is Miss Crawley right to see the army as only an instrument of social advancement? The status of George's death in such a context becomes more interesting when we remember from Thackeray's letters that he had strong feelings about the death. He writes, "when [Amelia's] scoundrel of a husband is well dead with a ball in his odious bowels," Amelia will find true humility, as we noted in chap. 1 [*Letters*, 2:309]. So this is a moment in the drama with a clear dramatic function for Thackeray — retribution for a villain, almost — and he chooses to present it in a multiply ambiguous context, one that ignores George's function as Amelia's hateful husband and concentrates on his role as morally ambiguous soldier. And we should note that these issues are raised only here in the novel, as if to cloud our responses with a fresh subject. To approach these multiple languages of evaluation with an attitude toward choosing the correct one is to destroy a complexity that Thackeray is working to create.

By undercutting dramatic unity and authorial rhetoric, Thackeray denies the reader the two fundamental tools for the comprehension of fiction. What we witness may be only accident; what we are told may be insincere, ironic, mistaken, the product of a narrow mind or a perverse wit. Thackeray asks for a maximal amount of scrutiny from his reader; perhaps he asks for more than his fiction can bear. Do these novels have meaning above the level of personal friendships, accidental history, and Pen's need to earn a living? We can spontaneously answer yes, but locating the source of that meaning is proving difficult.

Novelist as Preacher

Thackeray likes to preface his sermons with the observation that sermons are out of place in novels, and that therefore he will not sermonize. "Sick-bed homilies and pious reflections are, to be sure, out of place in mere story-books, and we are not going ... to cajole the public into a sermon, when it is only a comedy that the reader pays his money to witness. But, without preaching, the truth may surely be borne in mind, that ..." [*VF* 19; 1:280]. The sermon follows. By doing what the "novelist" should not do, he implies that he is doing something else. Why is a sermon out of place in the archetypal "novel," and how accurately can we describe Thackeray's methods as those of the pulpit?

Thackeray, like the sermonizer, is a fundamentally rhetorical writer, in that he writes not in terms of any abstract truth, but in terms of the reader and his response, and particularly in terms of the moral effect of his writing. To consider a Thackeray pronouncement out of rhetorical context is often to misunderstand, and to take it as absolute truth is to convince oneself that Thackeray is merely foolish. One such misunderstanding is a matter of public record. In *Vanity Fair*, Thackeray says, "An alderman coming from a turtle feast will not step out of his carriage to steal a leg of mutton; but put him to starve, and see if he will not purloin a loaf" [41; 2:306]. George Henry Lewes, in an article in the *Morning Chronicle*, took violent objection to this passage [6 Mar. 1848, 3; reprinted in *Thackeray: The Critical Heritage*, p. 47]. Calling it "a detestable passage," he says,

> Was it carelessness, or deep misanthropy, distorting that otherwise clear judgment, which allowed such a remark to fall? What, in the face of starving thousands, men who literally die for want of bread, yet who prefer death to stealing, shall it be said that honesty is only the virtue of abundance! . . . Of all false-hoods, that about honesty being a question of money is the most glaring and the most insidious. Blot it out, Thackeray; let it no longer deface your delightful pages!

But Lewes has made the error of taking the remark as pertaining to human nature *in abstracto*. As such, it would be morally hideous, since it would be amorality, simple pragmatism — one steals as much as one must [cf. the discussion of a similar matter in chap. 1 p. 26ff.]. But this is to ignore the message Thackeray finds in it: "If you take temptations into account, who is to say that he is better than his neighbor?" The lesson is not that all aldermen are potential thieves, but rather that we should take no credit for our respectable virtue, which has never been tried by adversity. Thackeray

repeats the moral elsewhere: "Oh, be humble, my
brother, in your prosperity! . . . Think, what right
have you to be scornful, whose virtue is a deficiency
of temptation . . . whose prosperity is very likely
a satire" [57: 3:175]. And, in a letter to Lewes, he
makes the difference in orientation clear:

> That passage which you quote bears very
> hardly upon the poor alderman certainly: but
> I don't mean that the man deprived of turtle
> would as a consequence steal bread: only that
> he in the possession of luxuries and riding
> through life in a gig, should be very chary of
> despizing poor Lazarus on foot, and look very
> humbly and leniently upon the faults of his
> less fortunate brethren. [*Letters*, 2:353-354]

In this sense, Lewes is like the little girl in Sunday
School who, when asked to explain the moral of
the tale of the Good Samaritan, said that it was
"when I am in trouble someone should stop and
help me." He has ignored the thrust of the rhetoric
and interpreted the statement about the alderman
as pure truth.

Thackeray's sense of the artist as preacher is not
a superficial one.

> . . . this book is all about the world, and a
> respectable family dwelling in it. It is not a
> sermon, except where it cannot help itself, and
> the speaker pursuing the destiny of his narra-
> tive finds such a homily before him. O friend,
> in your life and mine, don't we light upon such
> sermons daily — don't we see at home as well
> as amongst our neighbors that battle between

>   Evil and Good? . . . Which shall we let triumph
>   for ourselves — which for our children? [*Newc.*
>   38: 8:224]

His urge to sermonize is actually stronger than he
admits here. Often his sermons are not the natural
consequences of the narrative at all; rather, he uses
the text as an excuse to sermonize to heights the
text itself cannot support. Here are Thackeray's
reflections on Clive's preferring the company of his
friends to the company of his father:

>   The young fellow, I dare say, gave his parent
>   no more credit for his long self-denial than
>   many other children award to theirs. We take
>   such life-offerings as our due commonly. . . .
>   It is only in later days, perhaps, when the
>   treasures of love are spent, and the kind hand
>   cold which ministered them, that we remember
>   how tender it was. . . . Let us hope those fruits
>   of love, though tardy, are yet not all too late.
>   . . . I am thinking of the love of Clive New-
>   come's father for him; (and, perhaps, young
>   reader, that of yours and mine for ourselves;)
>   . . . Did we not say, at our story's commence-
>   ment, that all stories were old? Careless prodi-
>   gals and anxious elders have been from the
>   beginning: — so may love, and repentance, and
>   forgiveness endure ever till the end. [20; 7:309-
>   310]

The reflections are of a size and intensity the
particulars of the drama do not justify; Clive is
not a careless prodigal, and, though Thackeray
frequently invokes that myth as the pattern for

his story, it does not fit. Clive is a loving and thoughtful son, and, when Thackeray is less moved by his own swelling language, much of the blame for the Colonel's suffering is correctly fixed on the Colonel himself, who selfishly expects Clive to live for him. The moral is so attractive to the preacher that he will state it in defiance of the particular text. In other ways Thackeray's description of the cause and effect of his sermonizing tendency seems inaccurate. If Thackeray sees his sermon as a defense of Good in its battle with Evil, to insure its victory, we must complain that his commentary often obscures the clear division between those two elemental forces — in fact, we sometimes feel that the narrator feels called upon to speak out when the reader is getting too clear a sense of where Good and Evil are aligned on the issue at hand. Here is Thackeray's analysis of Ethel's treatment of Clive. Ethel likes Clive, but she is obviously destined by her family for a "great match"; she treats Clive with a provoking mixture of honest affection and cynical discouragement.

> I allow, with Mrs. Grundy and most moralists, that Miss Newcome's conduct in this matter was highly reprehensible: that if she did not intend to marry Clive she should have broken with him altogether; that a virtuous woman of high principle, etc., etc., having once determined to reject a suitor, should separate from him utterly then and there. . . .
>
> But coquetry, but kindness, but family affection, and a strong, very strong partiality for the rejected lover — are these not to be taken

into account? . . . The least unworthy part of
her conduct, some critics will say, was that
desire to see Clive and be well with him . . . ,
and every flutter which she made to escape
out of the meshes which the world had cast
about her, was but the natural effort at liberty.
It was her prudence which was wrong; and her
submission, wherein she was most culpable: . . .
do we not read how young martyrs constantly
had to disobey worldly papas and mamas . . .?
Does not the world worship them, and persecute those who refuse to kneel? Do not many
timid souls sacrifice to them; and other bolder
spirits . . . bend down their stubborn knees at
their altars? See! I begin by siding with Mrs.
Grundy and the world, and at the next turn
on the seesaw have lighted down on Ethel's
side, and am disposed to think that the very
best part of her conduct has been those
escapades which — which right-minded persons
most justly condemn. [53; 9:33-34]

Thackeray discredits the language of both arguments. In the first, the "etc., etc." is his indication
that gammon is being spoken, and the invocation
of Grundy is a sure telltale. The second argument
is compromised in subtler ways. This is a fine
example of Thackeray's habit of irrelevant dissonance. "Worldly papas and mamas" is flippant, and
"persecute those who refuse to kneel" is offensive,
but neither accomplishes anything more specific
in the argument than to put us off our ease with
it. Thus we may call such a method "ironic" only

in a very vague sense, since the dissonance directs
our attention to nothing particular beneath the
textual surface. There is conflict within the argument, but no indication of how to resolve it. That
conflict seems forced upon the argument by an
irrelevant intrusion. To this point we probably feel
we can choose between the two views of Ethel's
behavior offered, but Thackeray continues with a
final reversal.

> At least that a young beauty should torture
> a man with alternate liking and indifference;
> allure, dismiss, and call him back out of ban-
> ishment; practice arts-to-please upon him, and
> ignore them when rebuked for her coquetry
> — these are surely occurrences so common in
> young women's history as to call for no special
> censure: and, if on these charges Miss New-
> come is guilty, is she, of all her sex, alone in
> her criminality? [p.34]

Here the lecture ends, in irresolution. This is the
basic pattern of Thackeray's lectures — an argument, a change of mind, and a final turn of the
screw that reduces everything to uncertainty.

This process of the self-destructive sermon works
on a larger scale, between separate arguments to
opposite conclusions. When Sir Pitt has a stroke
and is confined to a wheelchair, Thackeray is
moved to meditation: "As for Sir Pitt he retired
into those very apartments where Lady Crawley
had been previously extinguished, and there was
tended by Miss Hester, the girl upon her promotion,
with constant care and assiduity. What love, what

fidelity, what constancy is there equal to that of
a nurse with good wages?" [*VF* 40; 2:279]. And so
on through a long paragraph, ending, "Ladies, what
man's love is there that would stand a year's
nursing of the object of his affection? Whereas a
nurse will stand by you for ten pounds a quarter,
and we think her too highly paid." Again, the
argument is a central one in the scheme of *Vanity
Fair*. But on the next page Thackeray tells us that
all the above is a fraud; Hester waits until everyone
else leaves the room and then torments the helpless
old man as a cruel child teases a kitten. Thackeray,
never lacking "face," now discourses on Hester's
*dis*loyalty in the great scheme of Vanity. Thus he
sermonizes on a text that he immediately identifies
as spurious — and proceeds to sermonize on the
opposite data with equal felicity. We can easily
imagine him sermonizing on the implications of his
having thus deceived us.

If Thackeray's preaching does not lead to moral
clarification for the reader, why does he offer his
text as a sermon? How do the preacher and Thackeray share a common approach to their material?

Mythic Archetypes: "An Old Story"

Ian Watt, in *The Rise of the Novel*, distinguishes
between the novel's illusion of unique reality and
the power of earlier fiction:

> Defoe and Richardson are the first great writ-
> ers in our literature who did not take their
> plots from mythology, history, legend, or pre-
> vious literature. In this they differ from

Chaucer, Spenser, Shakespeare, and Milton,
for instance, who, like the writers of Greece
and Rome, habitually used traditional plots:
and who did so, in the last analysis, because
they accepted the general premise of their
times that, since Nature is essentially complete
and unchanging, its records, whether scriptural or historical, constitute a definitive repertoire of human experience.[7]

In this context, we may note that Thackeray constantly relates his action to the archetypal pattern,
in legend or literature, that is its source and authority. Superficially, his language, the language of
the classically educated English gentleman, has a
habit of classical and literary allusion which reminds us that the events we are witnessing are
basically old stories. On marrying first loves: "Ask
Mr. Pendennis, who sulked in his tents when his
Costigan, his Briseis, was ravished from him"
[*Newc.* 62; 9:190]. On the disreputable company
at Baden's gaming tables: "There was not one
woman there who was not the heroine of some
discreditable story. It was the Comtesse Calypso
who had been jilted by the Duc Ulysse. . . . It was
Madame Medee, who had absolutely killed her old
father by her conduct regarding Jason" [28; 8:37].
The immediate drama is authenticated by appeals
to the mythic sources, and Watt rightly notes that
this is in violation of the spirit of novelistic realism.
This habit of literary allusion is little more than
the standard equipment of Thackeray's class. Yet

[7]Berkeley and Los Angeles: Univ. of Calif. Press, 1957, p. 14.

Thackeray makes the technique a matter of thematic significance by interrupting his drama frequently to discuss it, and its implications about the usefulness of writing what ultimately are only retellings. He begins *The Newcomes* with a "farrago of old fables," and his hypothetical critic takes exception to such tired material. Thackeray replies:

> What stories are new? All types of characters march through all fables. ... With the very first page of the human story do not all love, and lies too, begin? So the tales were told ages before Aesop; and asses under lions' manes roared in Hebrew; and sly foxes flattered in Etruscan; and wolves in sheep's clothing gnashed their teeth in Sanscrit, no doubt. The sun shines today as he did when he first began shining; and the birds in the tree overhead, while I am writing, sing very much the same note they have sung ever since there were finches. ... There may be nothing new under and including the sun; but it looks fresh every morning, and we rise with it to toil, hope, scheme, laugh, struggle, love, suffer, until the night comes and quiet. And then will wake Morrow and the eyes look on it; and so *da capo*. [1; 7:6-7]

And Thackeray keeps this fact before us by means disruptive to the dramatic illusion. A seduction scene is interrupted with a brief parenthesis: "(Surely the fable is renewed for ever and ever?)" [*Virg.* 18; 12:229]. And sometimes he breaks off in disgust and refuses to tell the old story over again:

Is not one story as stale as the other? Are not they all alike? What is the use, I say, of telling them over and over? Harry values that rose because Maria has ogled him in the old way; because she has happened to meet him in the garden in the old way; because they have whispered to one another behind the old curtain (the gaping old rag, as if everybody could not peep through it!). ... Whole chapters might have been written to chronicle all these circumstances, but *a quoi bon*? ... What is the good of telling the story? My gentle reader, take your story: take mine. To-morrow it shall be Miss Fanny's, who is just walking away with her doll to the school-room and the governess (poor victim! She has a version of it in her desk): and next day it shall be Baby's, who is bawling out on the stairs for his bottle. [*Virg.* 18; 12:231]

The tale has become rotten, like the curtain, with old age and over-use. And this reminds us of the techniques we observed in *Catherine* and *Vanity Fair* whereby the events of the text are validated by an appeal to the readers' common experience. "What is the good of telling the story? My gentle reader, take your story: take mine." There is a verbal formula which Thackeray uses to introduce this perspective: "Who does not know ... ?" or "Have we not all ... ?" What did Clive do when he met Ethel on the train to Brighton? Exactly what anyone would have done — what has been done by countless young men before — what you did when you met Mrs. Jones in your youth [41; 8:283]. The actions and events of the novel are explained by Thackeray in terms of general human nature; thus Clive is angry at Ethel for knowing Lord Farintosh because "nothing is more offensive to us of the middle class than to hear the names of great folks constantly introduced into conversation" [42; 8:299]. Thackeray's characters, like Thackeray, respond to events with generalizing moral conclusions; Laura responds to the news of Ethel's rejection of Farintosh's suit in terms of the Condition of England: "It seems to me that young women in our world are bred up in a way not very different [from that of Indian dancing girls.] . . . They are educated for the world, and taught to display. . . . " and so forth [59; 9:149]. Thackeray seems to have created a context for his fiction that allows the universal moral relevance that Richardson erroneously claims.

This is the main feature in which Thackeray's fiction resembles a sermon: its attempt to achieve universal moral relevance at the expense of dramatic intensity. The concept of a finite repertoire of human experience is, after all, an idea as much about art's proper purposes as about life's experiences themselves. The assumption that art should be morally didactic limits its subjects to the fourteen Deadly Sins and Heavenly Virtues; idiosyncratic behavior always exists — it is simply not worth art's efforts to record. The modern sense of art's infinitely diverse canvas is a change, not only in our sense of the diversity of experience, but in our sense of art's uses as well. Thackeray, like the preacher, gets his sense of art's limited repertoire from his assumption about art's moral didactic purpose. In these terms, Ethel's story has value insofar as it represents the marriage situation in England. For the preacher, the sin of prodigality is more important than the Prodigal Son; the lesson is truer than the vehicle by which it is taught. As we have seen, Thackeray's commentary is so important that, far from arising from the drama, it can force the drama to accommodate it, however much the drama must be distended. And, as we have noted, the dramatic action is of such little importance that when the Condition of Marriage in England is discussed as fully as Ethel's experiences allow, the novel ends without her marriage to Clive, the completion of the drama.

De te fabula

Thackeray's sense that the novel's truest object of attention is ourselves has more important consequences than his frequent whimsical instructions to the reader, that he take the book's lesson to heart — "Remember how happy such benefactions made you . . . , and go off on the very first fine day and tip your nephew at school!" [16; 7:265]; it also means that the responses by the reader to the text — his criteria for judgment — are always topics for discussion. For instance, in *Vanity Fair*, in the midst of Lord Steyne's characterization as a monster [47], when we have been taught to hate him most and take pleasure in the misery of his family, Thackeray interrupts to observe that our hatred is un-Christian.

And let us, my brethren who have not our
names in the Red Book, console ourselves by
thinking comfortably how miserable our betters may be and that Damocles, who sits on
satin cushions, and is served on gold plate, has
an awful sword hanging over his head in the
shape of a bailiff, or an hereditary disease, or
a family secret, which peeps out every now and
then from the embroidered arras in a ghastly
manner, and will be sure to drop one day or
the other in the right place. [3:6]

Thackeray turns our attention to our own dramatic
response, and its moral character — gratification
at our betters' misery. But it is not truly that which
we feel; rather, it is gratification at the serving out
of poetic justice to a villain of a novel. The distinction seems a crucial one. Thackeray is using his
own drama to "catch" us when we cooperate with
its demands. The device is common in pulpit rhetoric, one that utilizes the difference between the
easy, absolute judgments we make in experiencing
fiction and the more pragmatic morality of living.
The preacher will tell a tale of a deserter and then
ask, are we not all deserters from God's army? The
tale of the deserter, when offered as a drama, wins
an easy condemnation from us, at which point we
discover that the tale is not a drama, but an
exemplum, and that we have condemned ourselves.
But the preacher and Thackeray are playing a trick
here, since the relationship between the sympathetic commitments we make in a drama and the
moral judgments we make in life is not a simple

one. Our judgments in the novel are controlled
largely by our desire to share the dramatic experience, for one thing, and for another, fiction
often serves as an opportunity to exercise an absolutism of judgment life never allows us. Thus we
damn utterly characters for doing things we would
excuse or do ourselves with little difficulty in life,
and we take pleasure in being so uncompromising.
Thackeray is playing on a fundamental confusion
about the relationship between literature and life
— that fiction serves as a training ground for the
moral judgment. This error is furthered by our
having only one word for the very different criteria
by which we judge in fiction and in life — "moral."

An example from a simpler genre will make this
clear. The conventions by which we read detective
fiction are entirely artificial; we try to outguess
the author by reading those signs — for instance,
that the most suspicious suspect is almost surely
not the killer — and a good author writes using
those conventions knowledgeably, and perhaps
surprising us by having the overtly sinister figure
be guilty of the crime. But the drama and resolution
are in terms of conventions that obviously have
nothing to do with real life, and thus reading
mystery stories does not at all prepare one for
real-life detective work. And vice versa — no reader
of mystery stories would suggest that in life the
most likely suspect should be considered almost
surely innocent. And if reading mysteries does not
at all prepare us for finding the culprit in real life,
that unsurprising fact questions one of fiction's
basic grounds for self-justification — its use as

exercise for judgment and sensibility. Thackeray makes the same point when he turns from the drama to our judgment of it and asks us to notice the ease with which we condemn others in novels and excuse ourselves in real life, and to account for the discrepancy. There is, of course, an easy answer: we must only reply that the moral system of a novel is something quite separate from life's morality, and therefore there is no reason why the two should be comparable. But to say so much is to grant Thackeray his contention, that conventional romantic drama is little more than a toy and an indulgence of fancy, which becomes a lie when it claims more for itself.

We have been talking, in the last pages, about the uses Thackeray directs us to make of his fiction, and the assumptions about the status of didactic fiction implicit in those directives. We have seen that he validates his art by an appeal to universals of character and experience, that he will interrupt or destroy the dramatic illusion to make a point about the reader, that he leads us to see Ethel's courtships, for instance, as a vehicle to a discussion about generalities more important than the vehicle itself. But a qualification is necessary: this is the status Thackeray asserts for his fiction; it is not necessarily the status on which it really exists. As we noted at the beginning of this discussion, Thackeray claims his characters are vehicles to facilitate general discussion, but they refuse to submit. Ethel will win a dramatic commitment from us, however much Thackeray may suggest that we put her to other uses; and Thackeray indicates in his conclusion to the novel that he knows quite well the dramatic power he has created; there he tells us he refuses to marry Clive and Ethel, yet hints unmistakably that they do marry. That conclusion which refuses to conclude, which we have used repeatedly as the apotheosis of his rejection of the demands of dramatic form, is a sham, since he declares his independence and then quietly gives us the dramatic resolution he knows we need. We have been talking, then, in these last pages, not about the power of Thackeray's material, but about the author's assertions about its power, and the two seem somewhat at odds. It is, in fact, a sign of Thackeray's ambivalence that, when he says we all know X, therefore he need not describe it, or, this is not a novel, so you have no interest in knowing X — a description of X immediately follows. "How they were married is not of the slightest consequence to anybody": a description of how they were married follows [*VF* 16; 1:232]. These things are of interest to us, as Thackeray implicitly recognizes again and again. *Philip*, for instance, is an eight-hundred-page love story interrupted at intervals by Thackeray's assurance that no one wants to read a love story and therefore he will not give us one.

Most of the conflicts we have been looking at in these last two chapters can be contained, though not defended, in a theoretic opposition between the structural principles and artistic aims of the dramatic novel and the moral essay. Many of the difficulties we have encountered in Thackeray's style disappear if we absolve him of the responsibility of being consistent from page to page. For instance, in the matter of Sir Pitt's nurse [cf. p. 171f.]: Both arguments are of unimpeachable moral value; that money buys a loyalty in this world that virtue or affection cannot win, and that bought loyalty is insincere and based on quicksand, we would not deny — we would only wish that the two arguments not be juxtaposed so dissonantly. Put each argument in its own essay and publish them a week apart, and our objections disappear.

Thackeray's interest in universal didactic relevance; his emphasis on the reader at the expense of the reading experience; his lack of a convincing or even specified location in time and space; his use of characters representative of a class; his appeal to universal patterns of experience and the finite repertoire of morally pertinent stories; his stance as preacher, and his offering his story as a fable or sermon; his freedom from the dramatic present, and his destruction of dramatic suspense by the glance at the future; his obedience to a willful pen, and his stubborn defense of his right to be irrelevant — all these, and many more, are only disturbing in the context of a thousand-page work which is supposed to justify our reading it as a coherent unit and a progressively developing narrative. If Ethel is a vehicle for a discussion about marriage, she is probably not worth a thousand pages of dramatic presentation. And conversely, if she does justify those pages, it must be on terms that Thackeray's authorial habits obstruct.

Thackeray's theory of how literature has true meaning leads to the moral essay, while his experience of what literature is shaped like (and perhaps his knowledge of what literature would be bought and read) leads to the romantic novel. His lack of conviction about the value of that form leads him to hide from his novel behind an impenetrable irony, and his desire to make a work doctrinal to a nation leads him to obstruct the dramatic forces that assert the value of the story as a unique experience.

A sense of Thackeray's commitment to the methods and rhetorical aims of the occasional essay helps us understand his hostility to the conventional tools for the unification of the novel. Consider the famous bowl of rack punch at Vauxhall, and Thackeray's claims for it: "That bowl of rack punch was the cause of all this history" [6; 1:80]. That is another of Thackeray's jokes, claiming for his fiction precisely the features it lacks. There is a force of formal determinism working in the novel, but it is not one of act and consequence; it is rather a determinism of character or fate, which will out, in spite of the rack punch and all other instruments of plot mechanics, instead of by means of them. The rack punch upsets Jos' and Becky's plans to marry — but to no avail; the monstrous union is achieved anyway, though it takes years and a trip to Pumpernickel. There is an inevitability operating in Becky's history, which the events of the plot seem to postpone instead of hasten. In this sense, the plot of the novel is something to be sloughed off — in Gombrich's terms, it is the distracting flux of expression and posture that hides the eternal truth of the subject. The plot is rack punch — a trick of coincidence that obstructs momentarily the characters in their pursuit of their inevitable ends.

We will pursue this idea of eternal truths beneath the vagaries of plot events in a final chapter. But first let us determine where we have "located" Thackeray among his contemporaries. Beginning with a desire to explain the paradox of a thousand brilliant passages making up a whole of dubious quality, we located the force for disharmony in an extreme consciousness of the novelistic process at work and an extreme distrust of the moral value of conventional romance. His view of literature's moral value, which is basically an eighteenth-century one, is fundamentally antagonistic to his realist aesthetic, as we saw as early as *Catherine*. His lack of faith in his art leads him habitually to expose the artifice of his fiction, an action that is made more discomforting by the power of the realist illusion he creates and attempts to destroy. His insight into the processes of writing and reading would be entirely praiseworthy if it were not destroying a very compelling drama by its presence. An understanding of Thackeray does not lead to an understanding of his works, but rather to a full perception of the impossibility of locating sure meaning in the diffracted light of his self-consciousness.

In these terms we can treat a false sense of paradox that may result from a reading of these last two chapters: chapter 3 seems to suggest that Thackeray is an innovator; chapter 4 seems to suggest that he is a reactionary. Is he looking forward or back? Is he writing a new kind of novel, or simply not writing a novel? Our discussion suggests that to describe Thackeray as defending an aesthetic, either old or new, is misleading; rather he brings the criteria of realism and didacticism to the contemporary novel as he characterizes it, in the furtherance of a disquisition on the novel as an instrument of social and moral education. Thus he is more concerned with the implications of conventional romance's absurdity in the perspective of realistic assumptions than he is in defending a realistic aesthetic as an artistic Truth. Thackeray is, after all, confused; in the case of this author at least, that assertion must surely be something more than an abdication of the critic's responsibility. His approach is therefore a pragmatic one — he can expose the absurdity of what his contemporaries ask the novel to be, without offering an example of what it should be. His narrative techniques, which perhaps have here been unavoidably given the character of innovations, are in fact the techniques of his fellow novelists, turned self-conscious and with their implications about writing and reading made explicit. We noted in the case of the preacher pose that Thackeray does not invent it; rather, he uses the convention to spark a discussion about the novel, by noting the novel's inability to support the rhetoric of that image. So we would wish to argue in the largest terms: Thackeray is not best described as a realist; the illusion of realism we have observed him creating is a rhetorical device, by which he may give the lie to his own narrator's claims for an apologic orientation, and to which he can give the lie via his narrator's self-conscious responsibility of authorship. The conflict between realism and didacticism within his novels is a parodic examination of the same conflict that rages unobserved in his contemporaries' novels, and thus he is neither ahead of nor behind his time, but precisely at the center of his own age. His novels do not point to new horizons; rather they lead us to the very heart of the novel in the middle of the nineteenth century.[8]

[8]The Victorian novelist usually said to share Thackeray's self-consciousness is Trollope — yet how unproblematic is Trollope's self-awareness! When a pushy American woman asked Trollope how he chose the words when he wrote, he answered that of course he chose the longest that he knew, because they filled the pages quickest (Ruth apRoberts, *Trollope: Artist and Moralist* [London: Chatto and Windus, 1971], p. 56). This is superficially Thackeray's tone, but it causes us no problems, since it is safely ironic. Trollope simply means the opposite of what he says. It is merely a tease. Thackeray could speak the same words, but he would follow them with a chapter written on such principles and a computation of his earnings. He would demean himself and his art, until the laughter rings hollow. It is this failure of taste, in a man who established himself as a national arbiter in matters of taste, that makes Thackeray's self-consciousness more than Trollope's easy, graceful teasing. Thackeray foregoes grace, and forces us to consider difficulties with which Trollope is entirely at ease.

5: The Fiction that Is True: *Henry Esmond, The Virginians,* and *Philip*

Esmond as Art, and
The Virginians as the Recantation

We have argued that Thackeray, through his narrative devices, denounces the activity of his plot as only superficially interesting. The motions of his characters have only the appearance of significance; ultimately the plot is for "novel-readers," and an unpleasant necessity for an author who yearns to address himself directly to another audience. It remains for us to determine where, for Thackeray, the true center of fictive meaning lies. If Thackeray feels he must stand between us and the drama, denying us a strong involvement with the text by a whimsical disrespect for his own creation, to what is he directing our attention as an alternative of surer value? Is there a subject of such absolute validity that it is always presented in an unsabotaged rhetoric, which can be read without fearing an unseen mocking irony? When Thackeray's narrator turns away from his plot,

what does he turn toward? To answer these questions, we must consider *Henry Esmond,* Thackeray's own exception to everything we have thus
far described as Thackerayan, and his own response
to it.

Since *Esmond's* publication, critics have praised
it for being what Thackeray's other novels are not
— artfully formed and heroic of temperament. The
review in the *Spectator*[1] calls the book superior to
Thackeray's others "as a work of art," though it
adds that because of this it perhaps will be less
popular. Trollope, in his *Thackeray,*[2] praises the
book for its formal tightness. It has much of the
"elbow-grease of the mind," his only work in which
"there is no touch of idleness." It is "a whole,"
"its nail hit well on the head and driven in" [re-
printed in *Thackeray: The Critical Heritage,* p.
166]. The novel's characters are similarly praised
for being the alternative to Thackeray's others.
Mrs. Oliphant, in a review in *Blackwood's,*[3] reflects
the general opinion among critics that this is an
unnatural performance on Thackeray's part when
she writes of Henry Esmond, "The hero himself
is a hero in the proper acceptation of the word.
It is not the faulty modern young gentleman any
longer, but the antique ideal which Mr. Thackeray
has resorted to, in consent, perhaps reluctant, but
certainly complete, to the old canons of his art"

[1] 6 Nov. 1852, 25: 1066-1067; reprinted in Tillotson and Hawes, eds.,
Thackeray, The Critical Heritage, pp. 138-144.
[2] New York: Harper and Bros., 1879.
[3] Jan. 1855, 77:86-96; reprinted in *Thackeray, The Critical Heritage,*
pp. 202-216.

[p. 209]. *Esmond* as antithesis is also recognized by George Brimley in the *Spectator* review noted above: "[Thackeray's] fine appreciation of high character has hitherto been chiefly shown ... by his definition of its contrary. But ... the ideal is no longer implied, but realized, in the two leading characters of *Esmond*. The medal is reversed, and what appeared as scorn of baseness is revealed as love of goodness and nobleness — what appeared as cynicism is presented as a heart-worship of what is pure, affectionate, and unselfish" [*Thackeray, The Critical Heritage*, p. 141].

Esmond, then, is the unabashed romance Thackeray's other novels will not let themselves be. Though it would be incorrect to suggest that *Esmond* has nothing in common with Thackeray's other works, in the terms of this study it approaches perfect antithesis. It is formally rigorous, yet with no obtrusive consciousness of its artificiality. It is heroic, and its heroism is not compromised by the alternative rhetorics of an intrusive narrator. It is a basically unproblematic work, and has always been, from the time of its publication, the Thackeray novel best suited to a gentleman's bookshelf.

Thackeray goes to some pains to distinguish this book from his others. Verisimilitude is scrupulously sought. The narrative voice of Esmond in old age is maintained with a success that won praise when the book appeared, and which dispels any doubts about Thackeray's ability to control his unruly pen. *Esmond* was printed in volumes, in eighteenth-century type, and archaically bound; the title page reads, "The History of Henry Esmond, Esq. ...

written by Himself" and "printed by Smith, Elder, and Company, over against St. Peter's Church in Cornhill." Thackeray is telling the reader that this is not another Thackeray novel. It is a virtuoso performance, an exercise in self-control, consecutive narrative, and architectonic plotting.[4]

In the terms of this study we need not wonder why Thackeray would be moved to write *Esmond*. The urge to embrace the romantic ideal is one half of the dichotomy that governs his fiction. But why is the other half not operative — the half that requires that such an ideal vision be realistically tested, found illusory, and exposed? Though Thackeray has distanced himself from the novel as much as possible, it is still his. We can understand the writing of *Esmond*, but not how it could remain intact. The answer comes in *The Virginians*, *Esmond*'s continuation five years later. *Esmond* is consistently heroic within itself, but on the large scale of Thackeray's canon it is only a stage in a progressive pattern of heroic delusion leading to unhappy disillusionment.

The Virginians revisits the two branches of the Esmond family two generations later and finds the heroic age dead and the descendants of heroes playing out a jaded and pointless parody. Like *Rebecca and Rowena*, it pursues a successful romance beyond the bounds of the romantic form, pursues it until it runs it to earth in Vanity Fair.

The equivalences between the two books are easy

---

[4] Cf. Gordon Ray's *Thackeray* (New York: McGraw-Hill, 1955-1958), 2; 6:2, p. 175ff., for a discussion of *Esmond* as an attempt to be what the other novels were not.

to make. Harry and George Warrington are
brothers both trying out for the part of Esmond.
Mrs. Esmond Warrington plays Rachel, Esmond's
mother-wife. Madame de Bernstein literally is Beatrix grown old. The triviality of some of the equivalences suggests the importance of the idea of rein-
carnation to these peoples' existence. Harry enlists
and serves under Lieutenant-Colonel Richmond
Webb, whom Harry proudly reports to be "the
nephew of the famous old General under whom
my grandfather Esmond served in the great wars
of Marlborough" [62; 13: 415]. Little Miles, son of
Sir Miles Warrington, was born in the same year
as the Prince of Wales [14: 112], we are told without
apparent reason, unless we remember that in *Esmond* the Jacobite plot revolves around the fact
that young Francis, Castlewood's son, and the
Pretender are the same age. But clearly the equivalences are false ones; the players are not large
enough to fill out their roles. Miles's sharing his
birthdate with the Prince of Wales has no significance. It is precisely the unique feature of *Esmond*
among Thackeray's novels that there such a coincidence does have dramatic meaning; only in *Esmond* are features of the narrative thus artistically
determined. But not here. *The Virginians* lacks
such determinism, and Miles's birthday remains
merely coincidental without meaning. Similarly
Harry proves too foolish to be a hero [22; 12:
291-293], and George proves too cynically self-conscious. Madam Warrington is Rachel Castlewood
with Rachel's strength turned to tyranny, her
nobility turned to foolish pride of blood. All the

Castlewoods live without resistance in the grip of congenital vices their forebears handled with some elegance. "It's in our blood" is the refrain they use to excuse a fatalistic pessimism.

Esmond's influence is everywhere, but to no good end; attempts at heroic emulation become absurd. George uses the Esmond memoires as a schoolbook, but this new world refuses to provide opportunities for heroic action. Early in *The Virginians*, George, incensed by apparent overtures by George Washington toward Madam Warrington, forces a quarrel with him in the hopes of killing him. George tells us explicitly his model for action: "Do you not remember, in our grandfather's life of himself, how he says that Lord Castlewood fought Lord Mohun on a pretext of a quarrel at cards? ... I took my hint, I confess, from *that*, Harry" [11; 12: 141]. But the situation is hopelessly unheroic. Washington refuses to play a strong villain; he is a dear and trusted friend, instead of a wicked seducer. He is innocent of any intentions toward Madam Warrington, and only the most artificial and unconvincing plot coincidence allows George to convince himself of his suspicions [8; 12: 104-105]. But, most important, George's actions wear the outward form of Esmond's heroics to disguise motives most unheroic. When *Esmond* appeared, many critics objected to the unsavory nature of the relationship between Esmond and his adopted mother and later wife;[5] in *The Virginians*, Thackeray sets out to

[5] For example Mrs. Oliphant in the *Blackwood's* review: "Our most sacred sentiments are outraged, and our best prejudices shocked. ... " Reprinted in *Thackeray, The Critical Heritage*, p. 209.

remove all doubts. George's relationship with his mother is Esmond's with Rachel in its worst possible interpretation. Esmond is punishing a self-acknowledged rake who has attempted the virtue of Esmond's mother; George is infuriated at a legitimate suitor. He is explicitly "jealous" [pp. 82, 83]; his anger is at Washington's audacity to court, but more strongly at his mother's willingness to listen. Her considering another husband is a sexual insult to him and Harry, implying that they do not perform satisfactorily a husband's services. This first major episode in *The Virginians* seems to set out to confirm and intensify the element in *Esmond* which most endangered its heroic status. The duel is replayed, but the elements of the drama have soured and gone awry — our involvement is confused, no solution is satisfactory, and Thackeray simply aborts the duel, leaving a sense of incompletion and bad feeling. The gestures of heroism have survived from *Esmond*, but now they are at best unnatural and foolish, at worst a disguise with which a romantic hides from himself the distance between his romantic ideal and his own flawed nature.

Madam Warrington, too, is subject to a new kind of scrutiny. The tension between a professed saintliness and certain sexual and worldly passions is present in all of Thackeray's good women — Mrs. Pendennis, Rachel Castlewood — ; here that tension is dispelled, and the saintliness is a rationalization, the passions real and fierce. As with George and Esmond, there is nothing really new in Mrs. Warrington; Thackeray's perspective has only be-

come more single-mindedly cynical. Mrs. Pendennis is presented in the following rhetoric (from the
period of Pen's recovery from fever and near-forni-
cation):

> He felt himself environed by her love, and
> thought himself almost as grateful for it as
> he had been when weak and helpless in child-
> hood. . . .
>
>   There are stories to a man's disadvantage
> that the women who are fondest of him are
> always the most eager to believe. Isn't a man's
> wife often the first to be jealous of him? Poor
> Pen got a good stock of this suspicious kind
> of love from the nurse who was now watching
> over him; and that pure creature thought that
> her boy . . . was stained by crime as well as
> weakened by illness. [Both, *Pen.* 53; 6: 19]

But within the perspective of *Pendennis* Thackeray cannot recognize explicitly the womb imagery
and the unhealthiness of the relationship it suggests, nor can he confront the implications of a
"pure" and "saintly" woman "eager" to contemplate the sexual delinquencies of her son, or the
assumption that a mother's feelings toward her son
can be understood by thinking of a wife and her
husband. *The Virginians* provides a context in
which such issues become major topics of discussion. Thackeray is describing familiar figures in a
new voice:

> The truth is, little Madam Esmond never came
> near man or woman, but she tried to domineer
> over them. If people obeyed, she was their good
> friend; if they resisted, she fought and fought

until she or they gave in. We are all miserable sinners: that's a fact we acknowledge in public every Sunday — no one announced it in a more clear resolute voice than the little lady. As a mortal, she may have been in the wrong, of course; only she very seldom acknowledged the circumstance to herself, and to others never. [4; 12: 45]

Her sons refer openly to living under her influence as "slavery" [14: 46]. Why are Helen Pendennis and Rachel Esmond safe from this perspective while Madam Warrington is not? In *Pendennis*, Helen is Pen's guiding light, the absolute virtue whose memory is the final impenetrable defense against the forces of cynicism; Rachel is, in Mrs. Oliphant's phrase, the "antique ideal"; but *The Virginians* is a world grown old, suffused with the sense of time past, greatness lost, and a present decay of the spirit. It is a vision of Thackerayan cynicism made stronger by the memory of *Esmond*, and the palpable sense of that absence. The decay of the spirit can even reach back and taint the image of old heroes. Bernstein, Beatrix stripped of her beauty and glamorous expectations as she has been stripped of her romantic name, offers us a running reinterpretation of *Esmond* from the new perspective. When George complains to her of his mother's inability to forgive her son's independence, which she sees as disobedience, Bernstein replies,

"If Madam Esmond takes after our mother —"
"My mother has always described hers as an angel upon earth," interposed George.

"Eh! That is a common character for people when they are dead!" cried the Baroness; "and Rachel Castlewood was an angel if you like — at least your grandfather thought so. But let me tell you, sir, that angels are sometimes not very *commodes à vivre.* It may be they are too good to live with us sinners, and the air down below here don't agree with them. My poor mother was so perfect that she never could forgive me for being otherwise." [54; 13: 298]

Thus she expresses the feelings of every unsympathetic reader toward Thackeray's intolerable paragons. Because modern readers are uncomfortable with paragons, we are tempted to regard one characterization as rhetoric and the other as the truth; Thackeray's work as a whole makes no such simple judgments. After *The Virginians* comes *Philip*, a novel utterly dominated by Laura, the most intolerable of Thackeray's good women. Maternal solicitude and despotism, nobility and hubris — *Esmond* and *The Virginians* offer alternative interpretations of similar worlds, each on a different side of such dichotomies, each complete and convincing within itself, neither having the last word.

In *The Virginians*, the past is everywhere manifest; Esmond's portrait looms over the salons of both houses of the Castlewood line. In Virginia it feeds Madame's archaic and fastidious pride of lineage, while in England it shames the Castlewoods into more desperate dissipation. One family lives a parody of past virtues, the other a culmination of its vices. Neither works well, and we are left with no solution to the problem of living in the modern world with such memories.

This pattern of *Vanity Fair*'s perspective turned upon *Esmond*'s heroism is basically a pattern of desecration, and consequently *The Virginians* is Thackeray's least pleasing book. The memory of *Esmond* adds a new dimension of bitterness to the familiar bitter vision, and that format allows Thackeray some of his most daring violations of dramatic expectation and some of his most brilliant denunciations of fictive illusion. The novel is uniquely structured, in that its first hero, Harry, proves inadequate, and a new one, George, is brought in midway to save the book as a chronological action. The book's first half follows Harry's introduction to life and love in England. He is awkward and innocent, good of heart, handsome and strong. He meets a fine, simple family in which there is a witty and courageous daughter. He begins to run with a fast crowd. Thus, a typical Thackeray novel is begun. But in *The Virginians* things begun are rarely finished. This is the novel that begins with, Let me tell you a wonderful story about two brothers in the American Revolutionary War, and proceeds to spend its next two and one-half volumes amidst England's Vanity Fair society. Anticlimax is the *modus operandi*. Harry fails to be anything more than good of heart, innocent, strong, and handsome, and Theo declares herself of a new age of novel heroines by recognizing that her love was based on superficialities, and that Harry is a dullard. Thus we have a *Bildungsroman* which is

half done when we discover that, though the learning process is only half finished, our hero is too
simple to learn any more. Harry is unworthy of
his role in the novel: he is married off to a horrible
little chit and retreats to the background forever,
while George takes over the attention of the rest
of the book. An extraordinary turn of events, to
discover that the author has had the wrong man
in his sights for half a book, but understandable
in context: *The Virginians* sets itself up to be
another *Esmond*; it begins with a promise of battles, duels, and the other machinery of heroic
romance. In this scheme Harry is the brother with
the potential for heroic stature, because he is unreflective and conventional in his acceptance of his
culture's ideals of moral behavior. George thinks
too much, about his motives and those of others,
to suit a romance. For Harry, war is only a means
to win a gentlemanly honor; George looks deeper.
But the world is no longer romantic, and Harry's
unreflective turn of mind, which in a romantic
context might be a sure grip on the basics of ethical
conduct, is in this context unimaginative and un-
observant. George, unsuited for *The Virginians'*
professed first intentions, is perfectly suited to the
new world where the only refuge of the virtuous
intellect is in meditative misanthropy, and the
switch is made; Theo marries George. The cashier-
ing of Harry is foreshadowed by one of Thackeray's
best passages, in which Theo recognizes the distance between romance and reality. Thackeray
tells us that Theo has been expecting a white knight
on a charger, and has found she has got something
else.

That is in fairy tales, you understand — where the blessed hour and youth always arrive. . . . How should that virgin, locked up in that inaccessible fortress, where she has never seen any man that was not eighty, or hump-backed, or her father, know that there were such things in the world as young men? I suppose there's an instinct. . . . But they *will* fall in love. . . . They are forever on the tower looking out for the hero. Sister Ann, Sister Ann, do you see him? Surely 'tis a knight of curling moustaches, a flashing scimitar, and a suit of silver armor. Oh, no! It is only a costermonger with his donkey and a pannier of cabbage! . . . Sister Ann, Sister Ann, who is that splendid warrior advancing in scarlet and gold? . . . Ah me, he knocks twice! 'Tis only the postman with a double letter from Northamptonshire! So it is we make false starts in life. I don't believe there is any such thing as first love. . . . What? You fancy that your sweet mistress, your spotless spinster, your blank maiden just out of the schoolroom, never cared for any but you? . . . Oh, you idiot! When she was four years old she had a tender feeling toward the Buttons who brought the coal up to the nursery, or the little sweep at the crossing, or the music-master, or never mind whom. . . . If occasion had served, the comedy enacted with you had been performed along with another. . . . Lay down this page, and think how many and many and many a time you were in love before you selected the present Mrs. Jones as the partner of your name and affections!

.... I make no doubt Theo was feeling
ashamed, and thinking within herself, "Is this
the hero ... whom [my mamma and I] have
endowed with every perfection? ... He is
handsome certainly, but oh, is it possible he
is — he is stupid?" When she lighted the lamp
and looked at him, did Psyche find Cupid out;
and is that the meaning of the old allegory?
The wings of love drop off at this discovery.
The fancy can no more soar and disport in
skiey regions, the beloved object ceases at once
to be celestial, and remains plodding on earth,
unromantic and substantial. [22; 12:291-293]

And it is in *The Virginians* that Thackeray's most
emphatic rejection of the romantic occurs, in the
digression on the "rotten vegetable" with which
Harry plights his troth with the elderly Lady
Maria, passages from which we have quoted in
other contexts:

Two fish-pools irradiated by a pair of stars
would not kindle to greater warmth than did
those elderly orbs into which Harry poured his
gaze. Nevertheless, he plunged into their blue
depths, and fancied he saw heaven in their
calm brightness. So that silly dog (of whom
Aesop or the Spelling-book used to tell us in
youth) beheld a beef-bone in the pond, and
snapped at it, and lost the beef-bone he was
carrying.... Ah! What a heap of wreak lie [sic]
beneath some of those quiet surfaces! What
treasures we have dropped into them! What
chased golden dishes, and what precious jewels
of love, what bones after bones, and sweetest

heart's flesh! ... When some women come to
be *dragged*, it is a marvel what will be found
in the depths of them. *Cavate, Canes!* Have
a care how you lap that water. [18; 12:229]

Thackeray nowhere writes with greater brillance;
The Virginians seems to provide him with a vehicle
to say his best things, or his favorite things in their
best way, a fact that requires some explanation,
since *The Virginians* is a bad book — dissatisfying
in the reading, acknowledged as dried-up and dull
by Thackeray. Thackeray's career-long sermon is
here taking its most forceful form, and the badness
of the novel seems to help, not hinder. The explanation should by now be a familiar one — since
he writes about the failure of life to meet art's high
standards, Thackeray finds more grist for his mill
the more his novels refuse to be true to their artistic
selves. *The Virginians* fails to be another *Esmond*.
Without the memory of *Esmond*, the reader finds
it merely bad; with that memory, the reader is not
moved by what is gained in the reading, but what
is lost. Again, little Miles's birthday seems only
pointless; the memory of *Esmond* tells us that it
is really worse — it is meaningless *where once there
was meaning*. These two books together constitute
Thackeray's grandest monument to one of his central themes — the decay of idealism with the passage of time.

Thus there is a horrible, tautological propriety
to the badness of these last novels. To the critics
who point out that they are exhausted, repetitious
replayings of once vigorous and novel scenes,
Thackeray replies, And can life be anything else?

How many times have I told you this would be the end? Though these novels are not good art, Thackeray has left himself no escape from their particular badness, as that badness is the inevitable, irrefutable final document in his thematic argument. We need not claim that Thackeray set out to undo a mistake when he began *The Virginians*; as with *Rebecca and Rowena*, all we see is a desire for more of the same stuff as *Esmond*. The impression of romance being sucked into the maelstrom of Vanity Fair is very strong.

The argument *Ad Mortalitatem*

The change that *The Virginians* works on the pristine heroism of *Esmond* is repeated countless times on smaller scales throughout Thackeray's work. It is the commonest result of a digression. It is Thackeray's fundamental complaint about his plot that it cannot naturally contain this vision. We have said repeatedly that his whimsical abuse of his dramatic action is meant to redirect our attention away from the illusion of the dramatic present to higher truths, hopefully independent of the fictive illusion for their validity; the truth that Thackeray most frequently sacrifices his action to bring to our attention is the fact of old age, decay, exhaustion, and death. The fact of old age or death is the ultimate criterion by which the events of the dramatic present are judged; Thackeray's intrusions often serve to pose the question, Is our involvement in and judgment of the drama legitimate in light of the characters' inevitable death, and our own? This perspective, which we term the argument *ad mortalitatem*, typically allows Thackeray no flippancy, and to it there is never a response; when a digression, in widening gyres, finally arrives at the fact of death, there is a moment of silence, and the narrative begins again, as if it has heard nothing. The narrative continues unperturbed, but our faith in its claim on our attention is shaken. The narrative cannot handle the fact of inevitable death, and that fact bursts forth to blind the reader's eyes and disappear, leaving confusing residual images that obstruct the reading for the next page or two. Just as the narrative cannot deal with the subject when it has arisen, the subject cannot arise naturally from the dramatic context; it must intrude. The argument *ad mortalitatem* makes its appearance more striking by its very irrelevance. For example, here is Thackeray discussing the change that has come over Pendennis — in youth, the possessor of a fine amorous passion, and now a young man without the expectation of a delicate feeling, on the brink of marrying the artificial Miss Amory:

> Yes, it was the same Pendennis, and time had brought to him, as to the rest of us, its ordinary consequences, consolations, developments. We alter very little. ... The selfish languor and indifference of today's possession is the consequence of the selfish ardour of yesterday's pursuit: the scorn and weariness which cries

vanitas vanitatum is but the lassitude of the
sick appetite palled by pleasure ... : our mental changes are like our grey hairs or our
wrinkles — but the fulfilment of the plan of
mortal growth and decay: that which is snow-
white now was glossy black once; that which
is sluggish obesity today was boistrous rosy
health a few years back; that calm weariness,
benevolent, resigned, and disappointed, was
ambition, fierce and violent, but a few years
since. ... Lucky he who can ... give up his
broken sword to Fate the conqueror with a
manly and humble heart! Are you not awe-
stricken, you friendly reader, who, taking the
page up for a moment's light reading, lay it
down, perchance, for a graver reflection, — to
think how you, who have consummated your
success or your disaster, may be holding
marked station, or a hopeless and nameless
place, in the crowd — who ... may have loved
and grown cold, wept and laughed again how
often! — to think how you are the same *You*,
who in childhood you remember, before the
voyage of life began? It has been prosperous,
and you are riding into port, the people huzza-
ing and the guns saluting, — and the lucky
captain bows from the ship's side, and there
is a care under the star on his breast which
nobody knows of: or you are wrecked, and
lashed, hopeless to a solitary spar at sea: —
the sinking man and the successful one are
thinking each about home, very likely, and
remembering the time when they were chil-

dren; alone on the hopeless spar, drowning out
of sight; alone in the midst of the crowd ap-
plauding you. [59; 6:138-139]

The passage from which this is excerpted should
be read fully, so that the extent of its incoherence
can be appreciated. Though it is not at all clear
what Thackeray means, it is clear that for him this
argument does not answer the questions about
Pen's change of temperament, but rather oblit-
erates them. The argument progresses from Pen
to lost vitality, the insignificance of success or
failure, to the inevitable miserable death, a fact
that ends all discussions by making them trivial.
The hysterical tone (the galloping syntax of dashes
and colons adds to this) and the *non sequitur* of
the thought process increase the impression that,
far from being the philosophical consequence of
Pen's narrative, such interruptions occur despite
the progress of the narrative, and burst forth peri-
odically to overwhelm it. What presents itself as
a pause to dwell on the state of the narrative
actually leads us away from it, so that a wrench
is necessary to bring us back; there is no way the
plot's action can arise naturally or transitionally
from these thoughts. Sometimes Thackeray will
deploy his sentences and paragraphs to emphasize
the awkwardness of the *memento mori* in the context of the dramatic narrative. Here, Pen at a
dinner views a dying father of the family and
reflects: "In later days, with what a strange feeling
we remember that last sight we have of the old
friend; that nod of farewell, and shake of the hand,

that last look of the face and figure as the door closes on him, or the coach drives away! So the roast-mutton was ready, and all the children dined very heartily" [*Newc.* 42; 8:294]. Thus the paragraph ends. That is an unsophisticated example of a point Thackeray never tires of making: that our conventional perception of living a life cannot handle the knowledge of inevitable death; and Thackeray sees the conventional dramatic narrative, with its commitment to the dramatic present and to the concept of outcome in success or failure, as, if not the source of our perception, at least the instrument of its perpetuation. In this sense Thackeray's plots are full of people eating mutton with hearty appetites, oblivious to the people dying upstairs; Thackeray's intrusions as narrator force the fact upon us.

The intrusions often follow an emotional pattern that soon becomes familiar to the reader: a pause to consider the action, a *non sequitur* rush to broader and broader philosophical issues, a dead end at the grave and oblivion, and a return without transition to the action. For instance, when George Warrington pauses to consider his own and his mother's proud assurance that he or she is right always, he generalizes to the practice of nations, and concludes:

We appeal, we imprecate, we go down on our knees, we demand blessings, we shriek out for sentence according to law; the great course of the great world moves on; . . . we race and win; we race and lose; we pass away, and other little strugglers succeed; our days are spent; our

night comes, and another morning rises, which
shines on us no more. [*Virg.* 78; 14:192]

Again the issue has not been resolved, but steam-
rollered into insignificance.

Thackeray recognizes that such issues do not
arise naturally from the narrative, and it is one
of the main reasons why he has so little respect
for the narrative. At one point, after a long digression on how to live and how to die, in which Mrs.
Pendennis is held up as an example, Thackeray
pauses for a brief *apologia*:

Of these matters Pen and Warrington often
spoke in many a solemn and friendly converse
in after days. ... But as it is certain that if,
in the course of these sentimental conver-
sations, any other stranger, Major Pendennis
for instance, had walked into Pen's chambers,
Arthur and Warrington would have stopped
their talk, and chosen another subject, and
discoursed about the Opera, or the last debate
in Parliament, ... or what not, — so let us
imagine that the public steps in at this junc-
ture, and stops the confidential talk between
author and reader, and begs us to resume our
remarks about this world, with which both are
certainly better acquainted than with that
other one into which we have just been peep-
ing. [*Pen.* 61; 6:169-170]

Novel-spinning ignores a great truth for lesser ones,
a fact that explains many of the features of Thackeray's art. It explains the extreme repetitiveness
of his writing — the individuality of the particular

event only obscures the more important features
it shares with all experience: its place in the inevitable progression toward aging, dying, and being
forgotten. These truths can only be eternally
repeated. Also, it begins to explain the irregular
morality of the late novels, whereby the central
characters seem to become disenchanted with their
own novels and simply walk away from them,
whereby virtue seems to have been supplanted by
friendship as the fundamental factor governing
behavior. Both of these features deserve extended
examination.

Thackeray constantly tells us that he has only
one tune to play, over and over. "O my beloved
congregation!" he says, "I have preached this stale
sermon to you for so many years. O my jolly
companions, I have drunk many a bout with you,
and always found *vanitas vanitatem* on the bottom
of the pot!" [*Phil.* 2; 15:168]. This metaphor is a
permanent fixture in Thackeray's vocabulary, and
it accurately captures the experience — delight
without reflection, followed by boredom and nau-
sea through repetition. Stale is the sermon by now,
certainly, but the staleness of the sermon serves
a purpose — to warn us of the time when all life
becomes stale. Medium and message at times become perfectly joined, as Thackeray bores us with
repetitions of his message, that life can only be
repetition of once-fresh joys until they become
boring and tedious. In this context each novel plays
the same trick — it begins with the appearance of
individuality and freshness, and goes on to reveal
itself as more of the same, with altered superficies.

Philip seems to be a new book, Philip seems to be a new boy, beginning a unique life, but we find that Philip is Thackeray's British boy, that he is living everyone's life — and ultimately that this book takes place in Vanity Fair like the others and these people are all going to die. Each novel, except *Esmond* and *Vanity Fair*, is a *Bildungsroman* which traces a child's progress, not from *naiveté* to maturity, but from fresh idealism and a joy in living to exhaustion, decay, and loss of interest. The narrator speaks from a jaded old age to a hypothetical reader who is always young, and tells him his joys will fade. The narrator almost defines the features of his hero's world in terms of his own losing of them. Schooldays, for instance, are introduced as a time in which I can remember I took pleasure, though no more: Pen's entrance into Oxbridge is introduced in this way —

> Every man, however brief or inglorious his academical career, must remember with kindness and tenderness the old university comrades and days. The young man's life is just beginning.... The play has not been acted so often as to make him tired. Though the afterdrink, as we mechanically go on repeating it, is stale and bitter, how pure and brilliant was that first sparkling draught of pleasure! — How the boy rushes at the cup, and with what a wild eagerness he drains it! But old epicures who are cut off from the delights of the table ... like to see people with good appetites. [*Pen.* 17; 4:250]

Our interest in Pen's development is seriously challenged by the poignancy of the drama beyond the limits of the novel's covers. A familiar device effects this change of perspective in a phrase: "... this was the happiest period of Thomas Newcome's life" [*Newc.* 62; 9:188]. Thackeray says this about almost every one of his central characters.[6] The effect on our commitment to the drama is great indeed. Just as it is our inability to say this about ourselves that gives us a reason to get up every morning, so we need a similar uncertainty to keep reading a conventionally powered novel. Thackeray commonly uses this piece of information to disturb our dramatic sympathies; he usually says it when the hero's plight seems most desperate. Philip's struggles with poverty and in-laws are interrupted with especial frequency with the news that these were the happiest days of his life. "Philip — who is many years older now ... , and is not pinched for money at all, you will be pleased to hear (and between ourselves has become rather a gourmand) — declares he was a very happy youth at this humble Hotel Poussin, and sighs for the days when he was sighing for Miss Charlotte" [25; 16:120].

We are reminded of Rasselas, passing four months resolving to waste no more time in idle resolves, and upon perceiving his error losing some hours regretting his regret (chap. 4). In both cases the language is a telltale for paradox — in one who wastes time resolving to waste no time, or in one who spends his youth wishing and his later years,

[6] Cf. *Phil.* 29; 16:201; *Virg.* 75; 14:153; *Newc.* 28; 8:39, 39; 8:229.

with his wishes achieved (Philip marries Charlotte), wishing for the urge to wish — and, we can add, in a reader who expends his sympathies wishing to extricate the hero from his moment of greatest happiness. "You will be pleased to hear," Thackeray tells us with tongue in cheek, that Philip has escaped poverty — and wishes he were back in it. Again Thackeray draws our attention to something problematic in the way we read.

The fact that the moment of life's greatest happiness can be identified means that reasons must be found to live when it is past; thus Thackeray teaches us to live in terms of recollection and remembrance — and earlier, to live in expectation of a life of recollection. The error of not doing so is always before us:

> At this time of his life Mr. Pen beheld all sorts of places and men; and very likely did not know how much he enjoyed himself until long after, when balls gave him no pleasure, neither did farces make him laugh; nor did the tavern joke produce the least excitement in him. ... At his present age all these pleasures are over: and the times have passed away too. It is but a very very few years since — but the time is gone. [*Pen.* 36; 5: 156]

The fact is repeated with a redundancy hinting of obsession: Pen is old, and the time is gone; he takes no pleasure now, because the time is gone — yes, the time is certainly gone. Thackeray's interruptions often do nothing more specific than remind us of death in the midst of the distracting moment

— a superimposition of the death's head on the living face. After Pen's near-fatal fever, in the moment of the joy and relief of recovery, the narrator intrudes to turn the moment into something quite different: "he awoke calling out that he was very hungry. If it is hard to be ill and loathe food, oh, how pleasant to be getting well and to be feeling hungry — *how* hungry! Alas, the joys of convalescence become feebler with increasing years, as other joys do—and then—and then comes that illness when one does not convalesce at all" [52; 6: 14]. In the moment we learn Pen will live, Thackeray reminds us that Pen will die. There is a paradox about this view of death. Thackeray fears two things: dying, and losing the desire to live. His arguments usually treat both problems at once, as this one does. It argues, How horrible is death! Yet even more horrible is a man who does not fear the horror. The illness of old age is paradoxically worse than other illnesses because the patient does not want to recover.

Thackeray uses the fact of old age as a polemical tool in ways that imply that we do our best to forget it. His favorite argument against youthful passion is, look at the love of your young days now — she has grown old! Are you not glad you did not marry her! [*Phil.* 4; 15: 199, for example]. The argument assumes that such news comes as a surprise. Thackeray is in search of supports that do not crumble at the news — a love that can survive grey hairs, for instance. A love to survive senile dementia may be beyond his conception.

If the basic vanity is a forgetting of one's own mortality, Thackeray's style is the perfect vehicle to remind us; the potential for intrusion is infinite. In the midst of Philip's love struggles, Charlotte sends him secretly a "thick curling lock of brown hair (from a head where now, mayhap, there is a line or two of matron silver) ... " [25; 16: 122]. When Clive Newcome enters a tavern, " 'I am right glad to see thee, boy!' cries a cheery voice (that will never troll a chorus more)" [*Newc.* 25; 7: 404]. In the midst of nothing Thackeray pauses to note inconsequently, "We are speaking of old times ... when people were young ... when *most* people were young. Other people are young now; but we no more" [*Pen.* 52; 6: 13]. The novel becomes a struggle between the dramatic force of the youths' experience and the narrator's frequently overwhelming concern that, as these people are young, he is not. Just as Thackeray seems to write in search of a reason for an honest man writing a novel, so Pen scans his memories in search of a reason for living on. He scrutinizes the way the young live and tests their reasons for taking pleasure in the business with his knowledge of old age. The *memento mori* rises up before us, and we are as Harry Warrington, injudiciously involved in an affair with Lady Maria and plagued with the image of her false teeth — we cannot help seeing the grinning skull the flesh only slightly disguises.

What sort of values, then, can survive scrutiny from this perspective? A life is judged by the memories it has stored for old age. There is an

alternative side to the problem which is less frequent and more disturbing — a wish for painless
oblivion: "I can't print Mr. Philip's letter, for I
haven't kept it. Of what use keeping letters? I say,
burn, burn, burn. No heart-pangs. No reproaches.
No yesterday. Was it happy, or miserable? To think
of it is always melancholy" [*Phil.* 18; 15: 480]. But
typically memories are stockpiled like provisions
for a long, cold winter. Pen is usually careful to
tell us that the letters and other papers he uses
to document his novel have been meticulously
preserved by sentimental parties involved. When
George and Theo Warrington are struggling with
poverty and maternal disapproval, little Miles,
their cousin, disobeys his parents to visit and offer
his whistle to Theo's baby and a moidore to George
in his want. The baby is christened Miles — always
the greatest honor in Thackeray's world is to have
one's memory thus surely perpetuated — and
George tells us "his moidore has been in [Theo's]
purse from that day" [*Virg.* 22; 14: 249]. Touching
moments must be pressed quickly before they fade,
and it is usually assumed that suffering is better
than not feeling: "Ah, to part for ever is hard; but
harder and more humiliating still to part without
regret" [*Phil.* 14; 15: 390].

The best woman in Thackeray's fiction, she who
leaves the clearest memory behind her, is clearly
Mrs. Pendennis, and her achievement warrants the
strongest rhetoric: "All the lapse of years, all the
career of fortune, ... however strongly they may
move or eagerly excite [Pen], never can remove that
sainted image from his heart, or banish that blessed

love from its sanctuary" [*Pen.* 61; 6: 169]. But this kind of immortality and peace is the reward of a saint, and not for real people, Thackeray knows. What real people are to do to live, we must now consider.

Beyond "Poetic Justice"

The moment Thackeray's argument *ad mortalitatem* is employed, the conventional principles of sympathetic dramatic involvement, with their assumptions about virtue and vice, reward and punishment, are completely undone. Basically, the fundamental reading force — what is going to happen? — becomes an absurd question. We know what will happen. Similarly, we know what everyone's reward or punishment will be — death. The concern of Thackeray's enlightened characters can no longer be, what will happen to me in the end, but, how do I best deal with my certain conclusion? Consider the new morality in operation. Philip Firmin's first love is Agnes Twysden, a superficial, mercenary opportunist and the daughter of parents like herself. She encourages Philip while encouraging another suitor — Woolcomb, the rich, revolting mulatto. When Philip's father is ruined, Philip is rejected and Agnes marries Woolcomb. In conventional terms, Agnes's deserved punishment is obvious — she must be caused to suffer, ideally stripped of the wealth she sold herself to get, or at least taught her error in pursuing happiness in affluence. Punishment there is, but of a novel kind. She is miserable; she is physically mistreated by Wool-

comb; she is deserted by all decent people. So far
so good. But Thackeray, after giving us the features
of a conventional justice, tells us it does not matter
in light of a justice beyond the exigencies of fiction:

> She is alone and unhappy — unhappy because
> she does not see parents, sister, or brother?
> *Allons, mon bon monsieur*! She never cared
> for parents, sister, or brother; or for baby: or
> for man. . . . But she is unhappy, because she
> is losing her figure, and from tight lacing her
> nose has become very red, and the pearl-
> powder won't lie on it somehow. [40; 16: 415-
> 418]

Poetic justice lies in the fact that she is growing
old, and the rewards of plot development are insignificant before that dreadful fact.

What then becomes of rewards and punish-
ments? If they are not beyond the power of the
author to grant or withhold, as in the above case,
they become at least divorced from the question
of moral worth, at worst the comic manipulations
of a whimsical puppeteer author. The distribution
of wealth, for instance, because it is irrelevant to
the true center of experience, becomes material for
the most artificial parodies of architectonic coincidence. Philip needs a secure source of income to
allow the novel to end; Thackeray offers up, with
an emphasis on its convenient improbability, the
absurd series of events we described at the beginning of chapter 3. The plot is free to pursue its
conventional goals by any means, freed by Thackeray's perception that the assignment of wealth is

independent of happiness; the validity of the novel
no longer depends on the validity of the coincidental plot structure. The realistic validity of Philip's
experience is not jeopardized by the extreme styl-
ization of that ending, because we have seen that
Philip has met and dealt with the problem of right
living before it happens. The conclusion of the
novel has no place in Thackeray's thematic argument. The joke about Vauxhall's rack punch again:
the tyranny of coincidence proves to be an illusion.
Passages like the following seem to follow a different argument —

> O Mighty Fate, that over us miserable mortals
> rulest supreme, with what small means are thy
> ends effected! ... Mankind walks down the
> left-hand side of Regent Street instead of the
> right, and meets a friend who asks him to
> dinner, and goes ... [etc.] ... and just by that
> walk down Regent Street is ruined for life
> [*Shabby Genteel Story*, 5; 15: 76]

— but a deeper insight shows the consequences of
Fate's actions are only superficially important.
This passage, in fact, introduces the series of events,
complex and pointless, that leads a man to choose
between two identical daughters. Whether he
chooses Tweedledum or Tweedledee, his miserable
destiny is fixed by his character. Regarding the
walk down Regent Street and the poverty it brings;
for Thackeray financial ruin is usually a blessing,
since it rids one of the world's attentions and brings
the assistance and sympathy of loyal friends. With
a good wife, Thackeray's novels repeatedly teach

us, one can walk down Regent Street without
reflecting about which side one is on.

Without a perception of all this, one finds *Philip*'s
flippancy about coincidence troublesome in light
of Thackeray's career-long satiric campaign against
it. Consider: Philip, desperate for money, is hanging
on by virtue of his job as gossip columnist for the
Journal of the Upper Ten Thousand. Suddenly that
publication folds, and Philip is destitute. Within
one paragraph, in juxtaposed sentences, he loses
his job, catastrophe threatens, and Tregarvan,
M.P., drops by to tell Pen he is starting a *European
Review* and needs a sub-editor. Philip is saved, and
Thackeray is explicit about the character of these
events.

> "I knew it [i.e. that God would send help] at
> once," says [Laura], after Sir John had taken
> his leave. "I told you that those dear children
> would not be forsaken." And I would no more
> try and persuade her that the *European Re-
> view* was not ordained of all time to afford
> maintenance to Philip, than I would induce
> her to turn Mormon. [34; 16: 304]

A good Thackerayan joke, of course — he is drawing
our attention to the unsubtle manipulations of a
heavy-handed creator (himself) who does indeed
create magazines by fiat, that positions on their
staffs might keep his hero alive for three volumes.

Thus when the events of plot are divorced from
a novel's center of meaning, the plot is free to
degenerate into parody or farce. There are other
effects. If meaning is no longer found in actions

and consequences, characters become freed from
the consequences of their actions, and in fact freed
from the necessity to demonstrate by their actions
anything at all. If we compare *Philip* with a book
like *Tom Jones*, we are impressed with the difference between the responsibility the two authors
place on their heroes to make their own fates. Philip
does not earn his good fortune, either by actions
that bring it about or by actions that demonstrate
to us his deserving it. The forces of his undoing
— his unscrupulous father — and his salvation —
a hard-working band of thoughtlessly loyal females
— are independent of his character; the one gesture
toward a conventional pattern of error, consequence, and enlightment that Thackeray does
make — Philip's rough frankness — fails to power
the novel. As with Thackeray's other heroes, Philip
refuses to be enlightened about his "error," Pen
is never sure if the vice might not be a virtue, and
Philip is beloved for it by those who count. And
that loyal band stands ready to help Philip escape
the just consequence of his folly or vice. The
significance of this freedom from consequence is
most easily grasped by considering Thackeray's
single exception to the pattern. Colonel Newcome
suffers the just consequences of his greed for his
son and his malice toward Barnes; his desire for
the financial power to crush Barnes leads him to
shady speculation, and he is ruined. Mrs. Pendennis
and company swoop to assist — but the Colonel
refuses the help Thackeray's other heroes accept
without a qualm. He dies from the destitution he
insists on enduring, yet he insists, because he rec-

ognizes his fate as poetically just, and he will not
avoid it. The Colonel is a believer in the morality
of artistic form, clearly; Philip has not the slightest
concept of such a morality, where the judgment
of act and consequence is a moral absolute. The
Colonel provides us with Thackeray's one unquestionably right, artistically satisfying ending — satisfying as Oedipus's punishment is satisfying — but
Thackeray makes sure we recognize that such an
end is not inevitable or God's design or even the
author's; rather, it is the wilful action of an old
idealist, in defiance of more pragmatic humani-
tarians who can respect but not comprehend one
who would rather die in a tragedy than live in an
inartful world. The Colonel, in short, insists on
living out his novel; but that tragic determination
to make the rules of art obtain in life, Thackeray
makes clear, is the fond luxury of a past generation.
Philip feels no urge to demonstrate to anyone why
he deserves to be the hero of a novel, and no one
in the novel ever thinks to question his status. His
novel's freedom from the morality of action and
consequence makes dramatic tension impossible.
When Philip's hopes are dimmest, a large debt
suddenly must be paid; Mrs. Brandon tells Dr.
Goodenough, a rich philanthropic friend, that a
good lad needs money, and he writes out a check
[38; 16: 377]. Since the good Doctor's checkbook
is always within reach, the conventional forces of
drama cannot be generated. Moral forces have been
replaced with mere friendship.

This separation between the essential value of
a man and what he does has grave moral conse-

quences. In chapter 2, we noticed in *Catherine* Thackeray arguing himself from a proscriptive morality to one of relativity and tolerance. There he argues that circumstance makes a thief of one who "[was], and *is still*, an honest man" [7; 29: 133, my emphasis]. Whether such a thought is morally profound or merely meaningless, it is clear that, as early in his career as this, Thackeray is attempting a redefinition of character on some basis other than one's actions.[7] The problems that arise when one says that one who lies is not necessarily a liar, one who steals is not necessarily a thief, become apparent in *Philip.* There, ordinary moral judgments do not apply. Philip lies his way through a number of jobs for which he has no qualifications: he and his friends fabricate gossip for a column on European high society in an American newspaper; he then edits the *European Review*, publishing his own articles, full of ignorance and manufactured facts, in support of his witless publisher's political views; his friends urge him to handle a few legal cases, though he knows nothing about law. Concerning all this there is an odd merriment:

> We [i.e. Philip and his helpers] might write a novel. We might contribute articles to a daily paper; get a little parliamentary practice as a barrister. We actually did get Philip into a railway case or two, and my wife must be

[7] Biographical explanation of such a philosophy is not hard to find. Thackeray was a gentleman who was a journalist, which is essentially the same as an honest man who lies for a living. Thackeray had much to gain from convincing himself that a man could somehow be nobler than his actions.

coaxing and hugging solicitors' ladies, as she had wheedled and coaxed Members of Parliament. Why, I do believe my Delilah set up a flirtation with old Bishop Crossticks, with an idea of getting her *protégé* a living; and though the lady indignantly repudiates this charge, will she be pleased to explain how the bishop's sermons were so outrageously praised in the *Review*? [35; 16: 320-321]

Thackeray says of Philip's fantastic letters from European society — signed "Philalethes," "Lover of Truth" — "as nobody was wounded by the shafts of our long bow, I trust Mr. Philip and his friends may be pardoned for twanging it" [16: 284]. But that is just a nod given to a view of the matter that is otherwise studiously ignored — the view from the moral perspective of those upon whom such acts are performed: the readers who read the false gossip, those who listen to narrow-minded political propaganda tricked out with fanciful facts, those whose cases are pleaded incompetently by Philip, or those parishioners whose souls would be cared for by a faithless hedonist whose thoughts rarely rise above the level of the dinner table. The actions Philip and his friends take to help him are not seen as having any moral consequences beyond the circle of his intimate friends, much as we argued earlier that the charity with which Thackeray credits his ladies is a thing done by, but never done to, someone. These deeds are like stones dropped down wells; we are still waiting for the splash.

This tension between the reader's expectations

of moral judgment and the narrator's moral obliv-
iousness comes to a crisis in *Philip*'s big scene.
Philip's hopes of success have always been over-
shadowed by his father, an unscrupulous man who
may at any moment borrow money on Philip's
name. Finally, our worst expectations are realized.
Tufton Hunt, a loathsome character from Mr.
Firmin's past, appears in London with a bill from
the doctor, payable by Philip. Philip will be ruined.
Mrs. Brandon, his self-appointed mother, decides
to save him. She gets Hunt drunk, anesthetizes him
with a bottle of chloroform, robs him of his bill
and burns it. When he comes to and discovers his
loss, she denies all and calls a policeman to have
Hunt moved on. In praise of all this, Dr. Goodenough, Thackeray's model of manly Christian charity, says,

> Sir, I have always admired Mrs. Brandon; but
> I think ten thousand times more highly of her,
> since her glorious crime, and most righteous
> robbery. If the villain had died, dropped dead
> in the street — the drunken miscreant, forger,
> house-breaker, assassin — so that no punish-
> ment could have fallen upon poor Brandon,
> I think I should have respected her only the
> more! [38; 16:392. Except for "drunken mis-
> creant," his charges are apparently false.]

These are strange words from a healer. And this
is the deed around which the plot's success or
failure turns. Something has gone awry. Joseph E.
Baker summarizes the immorality of *Philip's* activ-

ities at greater length than we have done here,[8] and hypothesizes as to the cause. He argues that Thackeray, aging and desperate to provide respectable fortunes for his daughters, abandons his anti-social cynicism as unprofitable. Thus *Philip* is a sellout, and Thackeray's moral insensitivity is an insensitivity to the injustice of his readers' social class to others. In defense of this, he points out Thackeray's reinterpretation of the parable of the Good Samaritan, which serves him as the archetype for his novel. The moral of the Samaritan, Baker observes, is that charity comes from an outsider, whereas Thackeray's Samaritans are members of a rigid clique, and they are Good Samaritans to each other. Thackeray thus reverses the moral: it is no longer, look to those who are not of yourself, for they are your brothers; it is now, know who your friends are, and take care of your own, because good men are infinitely scarce. *Philip* then, is an ironic parody of the myth Thackeray constantly invokes as his model. But Baker mistakes this for a statement about social classes; Thackeray's clique is much more exclusive. Baker is closer to the truth when he observes that, whereas Aristotle in the *Nichomachaean Ethics* concludes that it is "our duty . . . to honor truth above our friends, " Thackeray would side with the drinking song which says

---

[8] "The Adventures of Philip," *PMLA*, 77 (1962), 586-594; reprinted in Alexander Welsh, ed., *Thackeray: A Collection of Critical Essays*, Twentieth Century Views (Englewood Cliffs, N.J.: Prentice-Hall, 1968). The page references are to the Twentieth Century Views text.

Ein Freund, ein guter Freund,
das ist das schönste was es gibt.
[p. 177]

But Baker assumes this preference to indicate a slackness of moral character, either through considerations of practical economics or through simple exhaustion and apathy; I rather think that such a preference is the necessary result of a career of hard thinking, and that, far from being a compromise with convention and a reversal of his career's values, it is the most radical departure from a conventional social morality his work contains. Thackeray has discredited the assumptions behind conventional ethics so successfully that he has left himself only the principle of friendship by which to deal with people; and if that seems a tenuous and feeble principle by which to live among people, be sure that Thackeray knows this; the late novels are full of the lingering sense that this business of life is not all that important. But, since Thackeray bases his fiction on grand ironies, we would do him a disservice not to note this fine one: his career essentially begins in response to Bulwer-Lytton's glorification of a murder in *Eugene Aram*; Thackeray's determination to cut through the glitter of style and expose the hard truth of moral absolutism cuts too deeply, and he ends up writing a book sanctioning a "glorious crime, and most righteous robbery."

The Christian Solution

If friendship is not of adequate strength to make life unquestionably worth living, where has religion

gone, that ultimate support of impractical ideals?
It persists, but as an exclusively feminine method
of dealing with life. Man talks to his wife, who talks
to God. The hierarchy is a rigid one. George Warrington writes of the power that sustains him, "The
gloom and darkness gather over me — till they are
relieved by a reminiscence of that love and ten-
derness which through all gloom and darkness have
been my light and consolation" [*Virg.* 81; 14: 244].
That love is not Christ's, but his wife Theo's. There
is no hint that such a supporting love can come
from a higher source. Thackeray's women, however,
do not look to their husbands as their husbands
look to them. Pen writes of Laura, "I could see
she was engaged where pious women ever will
betake themselves in moments of doubt, of grief,
of pain. ... They have but to will, and as it were
an invisible temple rises round them ... , and they
have an audience of the great, the merciful, untiring
Counsellor and Consoler" [*Newc.* 57; 9: 109-110].
And elsewhere,

> She spoke but seldom of her religion, though
> it filled her heart and influenced all her behav-
> ior. Whenever she came to that sacred sub-
> ject, her demeanor appeared to her husband
> so awful that he scarcely dared to approach
> it in her company, and stood without as this
> pure creature entered into the Holy of Holies.
> What must the world appear to such a person?
> Its ambitious rewards, disappointments, plea-
> sures, worth how much? Compared to the
> possession of that priceless treasure and hap-

piness unspeakable, a perfect faith, what has
life to offer? [*Newc.* 50; 8: 432]

We clearly sense that for Pen there can be no
thought of sharing this possession. Thackeray's
saintly women are like ghosts; their presence is
somewhat unsubstantial. Their distance from the
world tends to tip over into fastidiousness, like the
most anemic of the Protestant images of Jesus.
Madame Florac, for instance, when toasted at a
dinner party by her loving son, "returned his caress
gently, and tasted the wine with her pale lips"
[*Newc.* 76; 9: 375]. But Thackeray cannot taste
wine but he must drink deep; such an ideal can
only be for him what Helen Burns is for Jane Eyre
— an emphatic reminder that that road to salvation
is not open to him. Pen's admiration for his wife's
piety is that of a man who does not wish for the
strength to resist temptation, but rather to be free
from temptation altogether: not to have a saint's
heroic strength, but rather to find it effortless to
be saintly. George Warrington, with perhaps more
appositeness than he knows, compares his wife to
the lady in "Comus" — "Through all the rout and
rabble, she moves, entirely serene and pure" [*Virg.*
83; 14:256]. Those who manage to triumph over
the attractions of the world do so by failing to
perceive that they attract.

But if Thackeray does not seek true piety for
himself, there are definite benefits from living in
its presence. Pen willingly submits his cynical ra-
tionalism to the direction of a Christian optimism
that he admires but cannot hold himself. And thus

we approach a solution to the dilemma we have
contended divides Thackeray's fiction: for the fundamental character of the Faith he places above
his reasoned bitterness is that error which his
narrative techniques are directed toward eliminat-
ing in the reader — the naive assumption that the
principles of conventional romance obtain in real
life. Thus Thackeray finds life's value principally
in being close to those who hold to the idealistic
folly his reason can never accept.

Though Laura and Co.'s religion is, we are often
told, not the sort that makes any outward show
of itself, one tenet frequently makes itself known
— that pessimism is one short step from atheism.
In the second chapter we discussed the Victorian
misuse of architectonic structure within the novel
as a proof of God's benevolent order on earth, using
Kingsley as our example; Thackeray's women make
precisely the same use of the material of their own
experience to make the same argument. Thackeray's benevolent fools are all "novel-readers" in
the worst sense — reading is believing. Mrs. Lambert, in *The Virginians*, is typical: "Mrs. Lambert
was much addicted to novels, and cried her eyes
out over them with great assiduity. No coach ever
passed the gate, but she expected a husband for
her girls would alight from it and ring the bell"
[23; 12:295], and so on. But that same set of
expectations, in a slightly different vocabulary, is
Mrs. Lambert's religion:

> As for the women, the question of poverty was
> one of pleasure to those sentimental souls, and

Aunt Lambert, for her part, declared it would be wicked and irreligious to doubt of a provision being made for her children. Was the righteous ever forsaken? Did the just man ever have to beg his bread? She knew better than that! [79; 14:215]

The belief is the same, whether in aesthetic or moral terms — that life will conduct itself with artful propriety and obedience to the laws of morality, poetic justice, and dramatic structure. God, in this view, is not the archetypal Poet, but the archetypal Novelist.

As the Pendennis novels develop, they become more clearly experiential material for a dialectic between Laura and Pen on the true nature of the world — Christian-optimistic or cynical-misanthropic. On the subject of Philip's projected impractical marriage, for instance:

"Arthur, I am surprised at you. Oh, men are awfully worldly! Do you suppose Heaven will not send him help at its good time, and be kind to him who has rescued so many from ruin? Do you suppose the prayers, the blessings of that father, of those little ones, of that dear child, will not avail him? . . . "   Yes. This was actually the talk of a woman of sense and discernment, when her prejudices and romance were not in the way. [17; 15:450-451]

Pen's statements as a whole are ambiguous; he is sure that such talk is that of a fool, and that Laura makes life worthwhile. He does not attempt to state

a resolution to the paradox. But, although Pen is
unwilling to choose between the two sides of the
dialectic, one would suspect that the plot's action
would make a choice. Who, in light of the plot's
working itself out, is right? *Philip* particularly
seems set up to seek an answer to that question.

The issue is, should Philip and Charlotte, who
are in love and without the prospect of an income,
marry? On the side of sense sits Pen, observing that
love is excellent but that "a bottle per diem of that
light claret . . . costs one hundred and four guineas
a year . . . or to speak plainly with you *one hundred
and nine pounds, four shillings!*" [16:260]. On the
side of romance are Philip ("What you call prudence . . . I call cowardice — I call blasphemy!")
and Laura, of whom Pen says,

> When two or three little pieces of good luck
> had befallen our poor friend, my wife trium-
> phantly cried out, "I told you so! Did I not
> always say that heaven would befriend that
> dear innocent wife and children; that brave,
> generous, imprudent father?" And now when
> the evil days came, this monstrous logician
> insisted that poverty, sickness, dreadful doubt
> and terror . . . were all equally intended for
> Philip's advantage, and would work for good
> in the end. [40; 16:434]

The outcome should be conclusive. Will heaven
appear with sustenance and a respectable income?
Or will expectations of divine benevolence prove
foolish? The action of the plot gives us an answer
that is complicated, for reasons some of which we

have already considered. Help is ubiquitous and abundant, but it comes not directly from Heaven, but from those same ladies whose faith in Heaven's intervention is absolute. Philip is in need; Laura pressures her friends into creating a job for him; and Laura concludes, Praise God! Pen more reasonably concludes, Praise Laura. Also, while comfortable affluence does come in the end, by outlandish means about which we have said enough already, Philip has discovered a subtler truth that Laura's romantic vision expresses more crudely: Laura says, God will send bread to the righteous in their want; Philip learns that God sends the righteous joy in their hunger, while other tables groan in abundance without love. Here, then, is a reward independent of coincidence, whose probability might support optimism in a rational man.

Thus Thackeray finds two ways to justify his staying close to the romantic illusion his art seeks to cleanse from us. First, he interprets the fairy tale myth as a metaphor. No longer need the shower of heavenly coin and social stature at the end of the conventional novel be taken literally; as his good women preach that fable, it becomes as a parable in the mouths of inspired innocents who do not fathom its deeper meaning, as when the Bible speaks of the peace of being one with God in metaphors of wealth. With this perception, the fairy tale motif ceases to be only an indication of conventional art's failure to contain what we are witnessing, and becomes an accurate simile. George Warrington uses the echo forcefully when he says of his wife that she

bore *her* poverty with such a smiling sweetness
and easy grace, that niggard Fortune relented
before her, and, like some savage Ogre in the
fairy tales, melted at the constant goodness
and cheerfulness of that uncomplaining, artless, innocent creature. However poor she was,
all who knew her saw that here was a fine lady;
and the little tradesmen and humble folks
round about us treated her with as much
respect as the richest of our neighbors. [*Virg.*
83; 14:256]

A good heart does not win the Irish Sweepstakes.
Theo does not turn into a princess — she rather
teaches others to respect Cinderella for her virtue.
The transformation is almost as magical, though
the value system is metamorphosed instead of the
lady. Consider how different such an affirmation
is from a conventional narrative pattern, as exem-
plified by Dickens, where the magic works in basically dramatic ways, in terms of what happens. The
proof of poor virtue's goodness is that in the end
it will be transformed, into wealth or social status
— wicked men will turn into good men, and so forth.
Thackeray's reinterpretation tells us that such a
perception is fundamentally skewed: Virtue's
reward is that it is free from such vicissitudes.
Virtue is not transformed, but rather transforms
the world around it into something else, where
poverty is no longer misery and wealth no longer
a blessing. These moral ideas, by the way, are not
new ones, and they are not presented here as
important because of their originality or inherent

value. They are of interest because of the difficulty a novel-writer like Thackeray has incorporating them into the structure of dramatic narrative, and the implications about conventional novel form suggested by that conflict.

Second, Thackeray finds the romantic illusion true by leaving the world and living with a small group of similarly deluded good souls who labor continually to make their fancy real. God's benevolence shall be demonstrated, if Laura and Co. have to twist some arms to bring it off. The real world remains chaotic and artless, and it is explicitly forsaken. Aunt Lambert says to Harry Warrington, abandoned by society when his inheritance goes to his elder brother, "The world may look coldly at you, but we don't belong to it: so you may come to us in safety" [57; 13:339]. And Laura councils Pen in his struggles against overwhelming cynicism, "I must not pretend to advise: but I take you at your word about the world; and as you own it is wicked, and that it tires you, ask you why you don't leave it?" [*Pen.* 66; 6:264]. Here, then, is an easy answer to the hard questions Thackeray the literalist has been asking about art and life and the discrepancy between the two. Real life is not art — true, but a "real" life is not mandatory; if art is superior, live a novel. Thackeray cannot believe, he cannot even agree, but he can stick close to those who do. He chooses to be governed by a feminine idealism which is determined to ignore the real world to the extent the world refuses to cooperate with its ideals.

Epilogue

It has been the fundamental tenet of this study that Thackeray's work constitutes a major critical study of the Victorian novel's assumptions and practices. His method is fundamentally the exaggeration of conventional practices in the context of critical self-awareness, a self-awareness he achieves through the narrative techniques we have examined. His novels are best understood as archetypal novels of his period, annotated by the ironic insights of an obtrusive narrator determined to disrupt our involvement in the text, so that our critical faculties can be called into play — so that we may watch ourselves as we read, as Thackeray watches himself as he writes. As we have said, these works are dissertations on the novel, with a novel provided for discussion. The problems Thackeray raises, and the often unsophisticated level of the answers, suggests a severe limitation of vision about the possible forms and functions of fiction for those writing and reading novels at this period. At least as far as Thackeray sees, the novel as a valid human activity is seriously threatened by the asking of questions the answers to which are now such critical commonplaces that the questions rarely get asked anymore. That a reminder that the novel is fiction should prove so troublesome, is evidence of how much the fact was overlooked; how much the literature of other eras is compromised by that discovery, the scope of this study does not permit us to say.

Perhaps we should confess openly that Thackeray's grand iconoclastic search has a rather unspectacular ending. Morally, a search for true values which begins with a ruthless exposure of untruths finds itself in the end with nothing left unrejected except the love of those whose delusion was the first to be found wanting. Artistically, too, we must be disappointed. The search for a new narrative form seems to dissipate itself in a feeble sort of Idyll of the Hearth.

Finally, it has been the fundamental assumption of this study that Thackeray's depth and strength come from the tension between his perceptive, if literal-minded, criticism and an exquisite regard and understanding of what he is destroying to dissect. He is constantly in pursuit of an excuse to retain myths he cannot let stand. His best work is certainly the middle novels, *Vanity Fair* and *The Newcomes* especially, where the tension is most nicely maintained—where the puppets never become truly wooden, where the puppeteer's strings never completely disappear. As Thackeray puts it, voicing a favorite dilemma, "I never know whether to pity

or congratulate a man on coming to his senses"
[*Virg.* 56; 13:327]. That point is best made when
the excellence of the illusion the narrator is dispel-
ling is most evident.

List of Works Cited

apRoberts, Ruth. *Trollope: Artist and Moralist*. London: Chatto and Windus, 1971.

Auerbach, Erich. *Mimesis: The Representation of Reality in Western Literature*. Garden City: Doubleday and Co., 1957.

Booth, Wayne. *The Rhetoric of Fiction*. Chicago: Univ. of Chicago Press, 1961.

Ennis, Lambert. *Thackeray: The Sentimental Cynic*. Evanston: Northwestern Univ. Press, 1950.

Gombrich, E. H. *Art and Illusion: A Study in the Psychology of Pictorial Representation*. Princeton: Princeton Univ. Press, 1969.

Hollingsworth, Keith. *The Newgate Novel, 1830-1847; Bulwer, Ainsworth, Dickens, and Thackeray*. Detroit: Wayne State Univ. Press, 1963.

James, Henry. *The Future of the Novel*. Ed. Leon Edel. New York: Vintage, 1956.

Lester, John A. Jr. "Thackeray's Narrative Technique." *Victorian Fiction*. Ed. Robert O. Preyer. New York: Harper and Row, 1966.

Loofbourow, John. *Thackeray and the Form of Fiction*. Princeton: Princeton Univ. Press, 1964.

Mudge, I. G., and Sears, M. Earl. *The Thackeray Dictionary*. New York: E. P. Dutton and Co., 1910.

Ray, Gordon. *Thackeray: The Uses of Adversity* and *The Age of Wisdom*. 2 vols. New York: McGraw-Hill, 1955-1958.

———. *"Vanity Fair* — A Version of the Novelist's Responsibility.*" Transactions of the Royal Society of Literature* 25 (1950); 87-101.

Sacks, Sheldon. *Fiction and the Shape of Belief: A Study of Henry Fielding, with Glances at Swift, Johnson, and Richardson*. Berkeley and Los Angeles: Univ. of California Press, 1964.

Stang, Richard. *Theory of the Novel in England 1850-1870*. New York: Columbia Univ. Press, 1959.

Thackeray, William Makepeace. *Letters and Private Papers of William Makepeace Thackeray*. Ed. Gordon Ray. 4 vols. Cambridge: Harvard Univ. Press, 1945-1946.

———. *Thackeray's Contributions to the Morning Chronicle*. Ed. Gordon Ray. Urbana: Univ. of Illinois Press, 1966.

———. *Works*. 32 vols. The Kensington Edition. New York: C. Scribner's Sons, 1903-1904.

Tilford, John E. Jr. "The Degradation of Becky Sharp." *South Atlantic Quarterly* 58 (1959); 603-608.

Tillotson, Geoffrey. *Thackeray the Novelist*. Cambridge: Cambridge Univ. Press, 1954.

Tillotson, Geoffrey, and Hawes, Donald, eds. *Thackeray, The Critical Heritage*. New York: Barnes and Noble, 1968.

Trollope, Anthony. *Thackeray*. New York: Harper and Bros., 1879.

Watt, Ian. *The Rise of the Novel; Studies in Defoe, Richardson, and Fielding*. Berkeley and Los Angeles: Univ. of California Press, 1957.

Welsh, Alexander, ed., *Thackeray: A Collection of Critical Essays*. Englewood Cliffs, N. J.: Prentice-Hall, 1968.

Index

INDEX OF CHARACTERS